Practical Salesforce Architecture
Understanding and Deploying
the Salesforce Ecosystem for the Enterprise

Paul McCollum

Beijing · Boston · Farnham · Sebastopol · Tokyo

Practical Salesforce Architecture

by Paul McCollum

Published by O'Reilly Media, Inc., 1005 Gravenstein Highway North, Sebastopol, CA 95472.

O'Reilly books may be purchased for educational, business, or sales promotional use. Online editions are also available for most titles (*http://oreilly.com*). For more information, contact our corporate/institutional sales department: 800-998-9938 or *corporate@oreilly.com*.

Acquisitions Editor: Andy Kwan
Development Editor: Angela Rufino
Production Editor: Elizabeth Faerm
Copyeditor: Rachel Head
Proofreader: Heather Walley

Indexer: WordCo Indexing Services, Inc.
Interior Designer: David Futato
Cover Designer: Karen Montgomery
Illustrator: Kate Dullea

October 2023:   First Edition

Revision History for the First Edition
2023-10-05:   First Release

See *http://oreilly.com/catalog/errata.csp?isbn=9781098138288* for release details.

978-1-098-13828-8

[LSI]

Table of Contents

Foreword (...Looking Statement)

Who This Book Is For

This book is intended to be a sort of Rosetta Stone for enterprise architects looking to gain knowledge of how the Salesforce ecosystem works at a macro level. The aim is to explain what the components of the very broad Salesforce offerings do. It will accomplish this by utilizing the classic and widely recognized enterprise systems and capability frameworks as reference points.

Salesforce encompasses a large number of components, many of which have been renamed and/or rebranded over time. It can be very difficult to translate the novel terms from within the ecosystem to their popular capabilities. This book will introduce you to the vocabulary used in Salesforce and help you understand what role it can play in your organization, work, or learning journey.

The first and most critical point to understand is that the name "Salesforce" is a huge misnomer today. Salesforce started as a customer relationship management (CRM) tool. Then it grew. It now has a range of components and level of complexity that put it on par with Microsoft (and Azure), Amazon (and Amazon Web Services), Google (and Google Cloud Platform), and Oracle (and Oracle Cloud). Underestimating its scale and breadth will stall your comprehension. All the names and brands make it hard to figure out what's what. This book is your lifeline.

Senior Salesforce architects can use this book as an introduction to enterprise architecture terms and concepts, to help you grow into a multicloud enterprise architect. Some of the features, products, and capabilities evolving within the Salesforce ecosystem are composed of concepts that exist in the non-Salesforce realm, but that have evolved independently or been designed to act differently during their lifespan within Salesforce. Imagine having grown up with scissors, but never having seen a knife. In this book we'll be talking about taking apart tools like those scissors and talking about the pieces and how and why they come together—and maybe why they shouldn't.

Why I Wrote This Book

The goal of this book is to help you work your way into a new realm, by providing explanatory examples and analogies. I'll be separating the "market-tecture" from the architecture as best I can. No analogy is perfect, though, nor are they to be taken literally in every case; their role is to help you see the "edges" of a pattern and start to discern the underlying skeleton. If you are already familiar with the standard components of enterprise architecture, the shapes and outlines should make sense to you immediately.

Any and all definitions given in this book follow the same rule: definitions will be given for the purposes of this book, and anyone who quotes them out of context should be ashamed. In all seriousness, though, it is very difficult in the world of IT terms to come up with concise definitions without constantly adding footnotes and exceptions. Please treat these as attempts to illustrate concepts (architectural tropes) within the context of Salesforce, and not as authoritative descriptions. Also keep in mind that they are aimed at businesses and their architects who are looking to understand the possible role of Salesforce and all its functions in a traditional organization. Employees of Salesforce, sellers of Salesforce products, and various types of developers will have their own perspectives and definitions.

If you are not a hands-on systems-level architect, much of the detail in this book will not be useful to you. You can do a lot of Salesforce work without knowing how Salesforce works. If you live in a world of details, however (like security, licensing, budgeting, purchasing, integrations, or performance), reading this book will be worth your time.

What This Book Will Not Attempt

This book will describe some of the key concepts in Salesforce, but not all of them, and not to the same level of detail. I will be highlighting elements that help shed light on the shape of the ecosystem and may gloss over things that do not add to this. This won't be a book for the quizmasters that are studying all of the exceptions for exam questions.

Licensing is its own art and is best left to account representatives and sales teams. Prices can dictate architecture, so it would be wrong not to include pricing when discussing architecture. That's all I'll say about licensing in this book, though—there are just too many factors that affect "cost." Trying to write them all down would be an exercise in futility.

Implementation or practice details will be limited perspectives that yield insight into how something works (or doesn't) compared to another system/concept. The Salesforce ecosystem is growing and evolving so fast that only very broad or powerful components will be discussed. Every attempt will be made to keep up with new acquisitions and name changes, but be aware that you are entering into a very fast-moving world with many confusing and counterintuitive names.

With changing names and abilities, so comes changing functionality and fit. Some examples of good fit or bad fit will be given to help you understand how certain things work, but these shouldn't be taken as firm rules. As always, your mileage may vary; please make all purchasing decisions based on timely, peer-reviewed research and not solely on the aspects of items presented in this book.

How This Book Is Organized

The first two chapters of the book serve to get you oriented, covering the main application functionality and capabilities and basic terminology. The remaining chapters are centered around large domains: pillars of enterprise architecture like data, integration, programming, etc. Be aware that there is a great deal of overlap in those concepts in many of the elements of the Salesforce ecosystem, so you may need to skip around. It is highly advisable that you at least skim all the chapters even if you are only interested in one of the domains.

Since the chapters are divided by domains, the focus in each chapter will be on how particular Salesforce ecosystem components are relevant to that domain. For example, a data bus element may have a nascent scripting language associated with it, but our focus will stay on the data functionality. The scripting language may or may not be covered in a chapter related to programming. At the end of each chapter is a wrap-up summarizing "The Good" (everything the platform/particular components are doing well relative to other comparable industry components), "The Gotchas" (issues that might keep a component from being utilized for a particular purpose, topics that might be overhyped, etc.), and "The Growth" (what might be on the roadmap based on frequency of updates, history of added features, and acquisitions). These predictions are based solely on information freely available to the public and are subject to change based on industry direction and any number of other factors.

Discussions of individual components center around:

- What it is and why you need to know about it
- Contextual definitions
- Limitations compared to traditional/compared components
- Limitations within the component (to help you understand how to wield it)
- Missing features that might make you select an alternative

- Health/maturity relative to other components
- Adoption across the ecosystem
- Speculation and observations around Salesforce's investment in the component
- Likelihood of replacement by an acquisition

These observations are based on anecdotal evidence and should drive you to ask questions and prepare for lifecycles that could change rapidly. Your mileage may vary.

Architecture Versus "Market-tecture"

Be very aware that you may deal with varying types of conflation due to product branding not being aligned with actual classical architecture component names. Salesforce is no different than any other platform in that it is growing in a nonlinear fashion. It is not a simple product for a single use case. Be prepared for some confusion as you interact with people with different primary perspectives. This book will try to group concepts into pieces of a puzzle and show how they fit together, but lines are often blurry and names are inconsistent.

Mental Hurdles and the Best Features of Salesforce

As you study, if you get stuck, make use of the two greatest features of Salesforce:

The community, lovingly labeled the Trailblazer Community
> The company itself and the practitioners of the Salesforce arts are notoriously open and sharing. Teaching and sharing with others is one of the biggest factors that has contributed to Salesforce's rapid success. This culture of zealous multipliers makes it easy to find ways into the ecosystem, and the company enables and celebrates those who share. Make use of these resources, as they will accelerate your learning and they (myself included) love to share as much as they can. Pay it forward if you can.

Trailhead
> This is the branded name of Salesforce's training and testing playground, which is freely available to anyone who signs up and opens a free account. Salesforce makes almost all of its licensed functions available for anyone to use for free (adding some acquired functions/system stacks to the Trailhead offering is a work in progress). Did I mention it's free? The free orgs that you can spin up (you'll learn about orgs in Chapter 1, if you're not familiar with them) are called *Trailhead Playgrounds* or *developer orgs*. They are full mirrors of the real thing and even include some fake data so you can see how things work. You can get full exposure to almost every feature in Trailhead without spending a penny.

Also, please keep in mind that this book may contain future looking perspectives and information that may either have been only announced, previewed, rumored, or suspected, and which might since have ended up on the cutting room floor. Again, be sure to make any and all purchasing decisions based on Salesforce's published material at the time.

Conventions Used in This Book

The following typographical conventions are used in this book:

Italic
> Indicates new terms, URLs, email addresses, filenames, and file extensions.

`Constant width`
> Used for program listings, as well as within paragraphs to refer to program elements such as variable or function names, databases, data types, environment variables, statements, and keywords.

 This element signifies a general note.

 This element indicates a warning or caution.

O'Reilly Online Learning

 For more than 40 years, *O'Reilly Media* has provided technology and business training, knowledge, and insight to help companies succeed.

Our unique network of experts and innovators share their knowledge and expertise through books, articles, and our online learning platform. O'Reilly's online learning platform gives you on-demand access to live training courses, in-depth learning paths, interactive coding environments, and a vast collection of text and video from O'Reilly and 200+ other publishers. For more information, visit *https://oreilly.com*.

How to Contact Us

Please address comments and questions concerning this book to the publisher:

O'Reilly Media, Inc.
1005 Gravenstein Highway North
Sebastopol, CA 95472
800-889-8969 (in the United States or Canada)
707-829-7019 (international or local)
707-829-0104 (fax)
support@oreilly.com
https://www.oreilly.com/about/contact.html

We have a web page for this book, where we list errata, examples, and any additional information. You can access this page at *https://oreil.ly/prac-salesfrce-arch*.

For news and information about our books and courses, visit *https://oreilly.com*.

Find us on LinkedIn: *https://linkedin.com/company/oreilly-media*.

Follow us on Twitter: *https://twitter.com/oreillymedia*.

Watch us on YouTube: *https://youtube.com/oreillymedia*.

Acknowledgments

I would like to give thanks to (in no particular order):

- The Norman Public library for giving kids access to TRS-80 computers
- All the smart people that talked fast enough to get past my ADHD
- The University of Oklahoma for allowing me to inspire many of their Acceptable Use Policies (and never pressing charges)
- The architects in the Trailblazer Community that untiringly and charitably share their knowledge
- Accenture's CTA Elevate program, which has introduced me to a stellar roster of subject matter experts across many topics
- The Salesforce "True to the Core" team
- The entire Trailblazer Community, including the Dallas Salesforce Developer User Group

And the following individuals:

- Meighan Brodkey (my forever collaborator, rest in peace)
- Nathan Shulman
- Eric Shupps
- Eric Crew
- Andy Ognenoff
- Nate N.
- Rey Magdael
- Jenny Wu
- Kelli and Matthew Ditzler
- Richard Russell
- Brian Drevicky
- Nathan Kleffman
- Moyez Thanawalla
- Rodrigo Cruz
- Jon Busman
- Scott Herson
- Stephan Chandler-Garcia
- Ted Wehner
- Derek Bumpas
- Logan Cox
- Steve Linehan
- Drew Minkin
- Joshua Bennett
- Robert Kelly
- Ms. Mayhen
- Mrs. Gatewood

Finally, a special thanks to my parents for letting me take apart all my toys and tie up the phone lines all night on the modem; and to my loving wife.

CHAPTER 1

Main Application Functionality and Capabilities

It's really hard to understand an ecosystem without establishing some boundaries and definitions. As a systems person, I will frequently refer to things *inside* and *outside* of a virtual ecosystem. The terms are fluid. Branding often overlaps with functionality. From a practitioner's standpoint, you may not clearly see where the edges are, and over time those edges will become even less perceivable. I will try to explain what type of "inside" and "outside" I am referring to as we go. Be ready to dump out your glass and reset as you read.

These first chapters will focus more on defining the boundary concepts than teaching where or how to use them. Once you know that the bowl contains milk and not white paint, you should know what to do with it. By the end of this chapter, you should have a decent frame of reference for further learning. The outline of the whole Salesforce ecosystem should be clear, and you should have some understanding of the depth of its capabilities.

Salesforce and Clouds

When learning about the Salesforce ecosystem, the first rule is to set aside your preconceptions about a lot of terminology. *Cloud* is one of the most egregiously misused terms in all of modern IT, and it's a very polymorphic term inside the ecosystem. Learning to put a special fnord around any specific definition is essential to absorbing the many paradigms represented within it.

Salesforce started out as a web-based application like Google's Gmail. (Analogy #1, and we're off to the races.) What does that mean? We can clarify by listing its basic functions/capabilities (Table 1-1).

Table 1-1. Basic features of Gmail

1 Access from the internet/anywhere
2 Compose messages
3 Send messages
4 Receive messages
5 Store messages
6 Delete messages
7 Keep a list of people you send to
8 Provide security/track logins per user
9 My email doesn't interfere with your email

The Salesforce customer relationship management (CRM) system got quite good at all of those functions—so good that it handled them better than the rest of the industry, with more basic platforms. The Salesforce CRM grew up in the early cloud, whereas every other competitor was very much "stuck" to an unshared hardware model.

Let's do our first Rosetta Stone comparison with a Gmail to Salesforce matchup (Table 1-2).

Table 1-2. Comparing Gmail features to Salesforce CRM features (capabilities)

	Gmail example	Salesforce CRM
1	Accessed from the internet/anywhere	Yup
2	Compose messages	Enter data
3	Send messages	Share with others
4	Receive messages	View data from others
5	Store messages	Store data in a database
6	Delete messages	Manage data
7	My email doesn't interfere with your email	Multitenancy
8	Provide security/track logins per user	Yes
9	Keep a list of people you send to	CRM functionality

If you remove the last part, the CRM functions, and leave the skeleton of the data, display, and automation platform, you have the Lightning Platform (Table 1-3). This is the name for the basic Salesforce platform minus any licensed extras. It's also known as the Customer 360 Platform. The sales-related functions are available via the Sales Cloud platform.

Table 1-3. Salesforce Lightning Platform/Sales Cloud features

	Gmail example	Salesforce CRM	Salesforce product
1	Accessed from the internet/anywhere	Yup	Lightning Platform
2	Compose messages	Enter data	
3	Send messages	Share with others	
4	Receive messages	View data from others	
5	Store messages	Store data in a database	
6	Delete messages	Manage data	
7	My email doesn't interfere with your email	Multitenancy	
8	Provide security/track logins per user	Yes	
9	Keep a list of people you send to	CRM functionality	Sales Cloud

The removal of the Sales Cloud functions (and other function-specific features included in the various other ecosystem components) leaves a very capable framework for building and deploying scalable cloud-based applications.

What's in a Name?

This brings us to our first set of clarifications. Ever since Salesforce gained popularity with a platform that doesn't have anything to do with "sales," it's started to live in the shadow of its own name. This identity problem has been looming for the last few decades.

Colloquially, "Salesforce" can mean three different things:

- The company cofounded by Marc Benioff and all its holdings
- The platform that most of the internally developed products live on
- The Sales Cloud functionality (the initial seed of all three, which lives on the Salesforce platform and is managed by the company called Salesforce)

Salesforce today includes functionality that is useful across many different industries beyond sales, service, and marketing. Those were some of its earliest industry alignments, but it would be difficult to find an industry today that is *not* using Salesforce for something.

This brings us to our second important clarification. *Cloud* in the Salesforce lexicon doesn't always mean a separate hosting location. Salesforce tools and services like Sales Cloud and Service Cloud are add-on packages that you can license and have installed/enabled on your platform instance (that is, the server or cluster of servers your version of Salesforce is hosted on).

The effort to distinguish all of its sub-brands and clarify what function lives under what moniker has been episodic, so watch for major brands/trademarks like Lightning, Einstein, CRM, and 360, all of which have shifting meanings and connotations.

It makes sense if you consider it from a layered and evolutionary perspective, but you'll have to let the constant renaming wash over you. I think I prefer it to the acronym soup found in other platforms!

To see how the Salesforce ecosystem offerings compare to other cloud providers, let's start with the overview in Figure 1-1 and a simple definition of a cloud: "A cloud is the net sum of internet-accessible hosted services provided by a company that can be used by people or businesses outside of that company." This figure puts some of Salesforce's offerings in context with other providers that you might have worked with already. Salesforce is best known for its software as a service (SaaS) application for salespeople but also has a platform as a service (PaaS) offering and owns a full cloud service provider called Heroku that has capabilities similar to other big names in the industry.

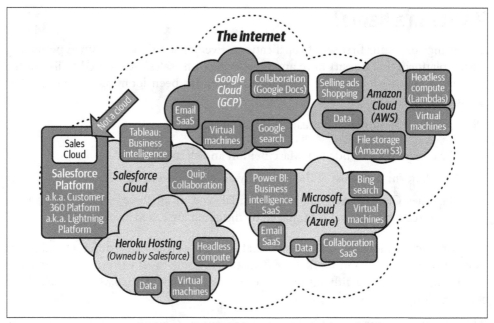

Figure 1-1. An assortment of cloud providers

Let's zoom in on the "Salesforce Cloud" section of that diagram and distinguish between the applications and the platform (Figure 1-2). (If you're not already familiar with cloud infrastructure concepts, skip ahead to Figure 2-3 in the next chapter for a basic list of ingredients.)

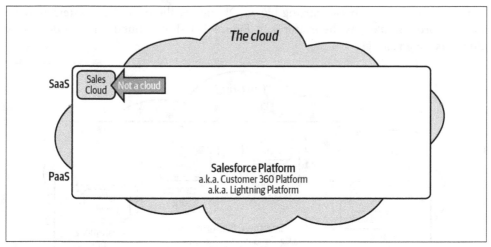

Figure 1-2. Clouds, PaaS, and SaaS

Sales Cloud is a package of functionality that is enabled for your instance of Sales-force—that is, the instance your *organization*, or *org*, resides on. (In Salesforce, the terms "instance" and "org" are often used interchangeably.)

When you log in to your instance, you can make use of the basic platform features as well as any additional features for which you have purchased licenses (Figure 1-3).

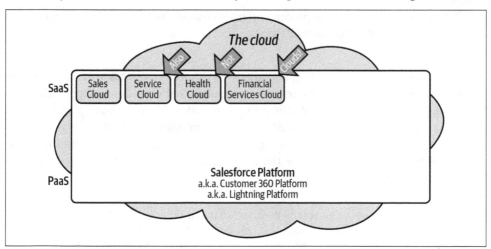

Figure 1-3. Clouds and not clouds

You can use this as a basic starting block. Of course, the overall ecosystem may be much more complex, as the example in Figure 1-4 shows, but I'll try to demystify things as we go along.

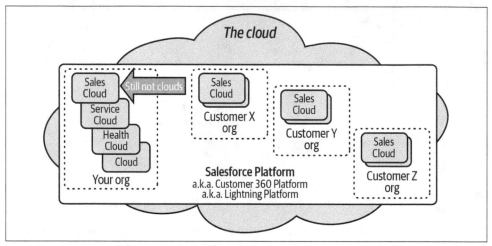

Figure 1-4. Company orgs and features

Here are some definitions and conventions we'll be using going forward:

Salesforce cloud

    This is the sum total of all product offerings owned by the Salesforce corporation offered off-premises as SaaS or PaaS.

Salesforce instance

    This is a multitenant hosting container that shares resources with multiple clients. This is a logical container of many systems that provides services. Salesforce applies updates per instance, in groups of instances that could also be called instances (Salesforce has trended toward calling these units of shared resources *pods*). You can infer some of the bigger system management groupings by looking at the Salesforce Trust site (*https://trust.salesforce.com*), where the company openly reports on issues and patches.

You may be on several pods for what you think is a single org. Your pod may host features that you don't use in your org. The concept of a pod only ever matters to a customer for update timings and outages.

Salesforce org

Salesforce has more customers hosted than it has servers. Salesforce servers/services are multitenant. The server infrastructure is behind the curtain and known to few. For the purposes of security, administration, and architecture, a Salesforce instance is something that can have a unique URL. This will be explained in more detail later, but for the most part when we refer to an *org* we mean the specific logical application service boundaries tied to you as a company/customer. Patches to an instance affect all orgs on that instance. More on this later.

Product or feature

This is a named/branded piece of functionality that may or may not be able to coexist with other products in the same instance.

Sandbox

This is a copy of the "main" production org, with the same features and a limited and scopable amount of the data. In Salesforce, the production org is the parent of all the lower orgs, like dev and test. Sandboxes get their own URLs and technically run on separate hardware hosts than the production org, but they are logically connected to and managed from that org. Sandbox orgs should be considered separate from your production org *only* with relation to direct performance. Most other aspects are linked up to production.

If anything covered in this chapter isn't clear, please stop, reread, and pay special attention to the diagrams. Still not crystal? Do some googling and phone a friend to make sure you grok all of these logical boundaries. With the exception of pods, you'll need to be fluent in all of these concepts to work at the enterprise level with Salesforce. It's not just one thing, and it really is "bigger on the inside." In the next chapters, we will start slicing the boundaries and defining new dimensions for different types of boundaries.

CHAPTER 2

How It All Works

Now that you have a handle on all the basic terminology, we'll dive a little deeper into the technical components. Salesforce concepts and products are getting unified and renamed all the time, so please be aware that some of the names you see here may be incorrect, depending on when you read this.

We will be focusing on the soft "virtual" tiers of the platform and some of the untouchable real tiers in this chapter. Some of the underlying systems may not be directly accessible or available for use in their classic sense (by end users or administrators). For example, the underlying database system in Salesforce is powered by Oracle, but you can't write stored procedures for it or use native Structured Query Language (SQL); Oracle is behind the curtain. You'll need to pay attention to the caveats, but knowing what they are will help you understand the connected functionality.

Basic Concepts of the "Full Stack"

If you're familiar with the concept of full stack development, this won't be new to you. Basically, at any layer of the stack, you can have functions, code, or customization. As Figure 2-1 shows, there are layers that can be customized (unlocked) and others that cannot (locked). The data and many configurations are accessible through a variety of APIs and user interfaces. This is another highly simplified referential diagram; there is a lot of nuance to each of these layers, and we will drill into many of them later in this book.

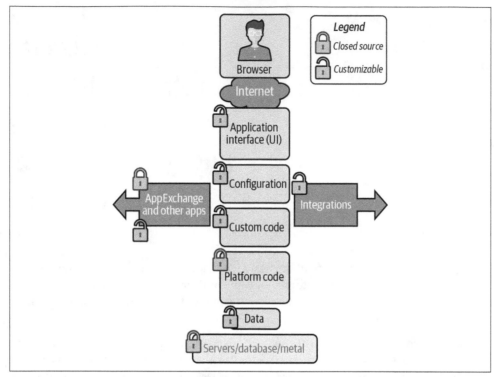

Figure 2-1. A simplified Open Systems Interconnection (OSI) model for continued skeletal explanations

Each of the Salesforce "stacks" has its own version of the sections from the UI down to the data. The metal-tier resources are distributed as needed, and with the advent of Hyperforce (discussed later in this chapter) Salesforce is moving its workloads to Amazon Web Services (AWS). As with pods, you won't ever really need to know the details of that. However, you will need to understand these distinctions to identify the locations of different features. Some features only exist at the data layer, some only in platform code, and others could be platform code add-ins. For all intents and purposes, the servers and database servers are fully behind the curtain and inaccessible.

Basic Product Stacks

There are multiple Salesforce (the company)-acquired technology stacks that are in play when we talk about "Salesforce" architecture. We will mostly be discussing the components mentioned in the foreword that make up the main vertical of Salesforce functions and hosting. Over time these lines will continue to blur due to changes in product names and new additions to the Salesforce core stack (Figure 2-2). You may not be allowed to see them, and in most cases you won't need to.

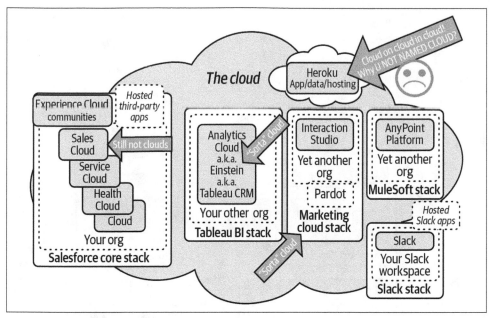

Figure 2-2. Stacks and "clouds"

Everything in this figure is owned by the Salesforce corporation and part of the Salesforce ecosystem. They're effectively different technology stacks, with varying levels of integration with one another (and varying levels of smoothness to those integrations). For most of this book, we will be discussing the Salesforce core stack, and I'll reference anything that is outside of that box by its name (du jour). For example, Vlocity is a recent acquisition by Salesforce. Effectively, it is functionality that gets added to "your org" in the Salesforce core stack. This is not a comprehensive diagram, but it should at least give you some idea of what goes where and how things fit together.

Figure 2-3 provides a very high-level representation of cloud service capabilities. The base units of file storage, structured data, and compute are present across all cloud (PaaS and SaaS) service providers. The boxes are specific services based on one or (where they overlap) a combination of the core resource types. One of the assumptions of working "in the cloud" is that access/transfer is a given, but there is a cost and you will be paying for it somewhere. Since your consumption might be variable based on time, ad placement, season, events, or other patterns, you will probably be paying based on some averaged measure like "user count," or by CPU time/load or data transfers. (*CPU* or *compute* refers to the processing of data or calculations, as distinct from storing data. Bitcoin mining and data decryption algorithms are some purist examples of highly mathematical workloads that do not require much access to data.) Each cloud provider will be metering resource consumption and charging you for those resources in some way.

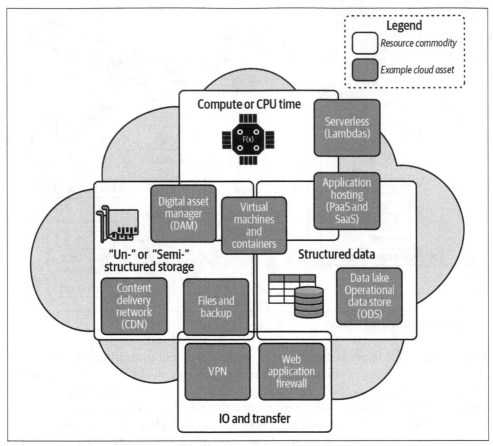

Figure 2-3. The resources you are renting in a cloud

Physical Systems and Infrastructure Concepts

Let's dive into the bigger-picture concepts that will help you understand how the blocks are assembled. *Physical* is an interesting distinction to make in a SaaS/PaaS ecosystem because for the most part you never get to see the physical systems, just the exposed web or API interfaces. The distinction of a physical boundary means that you cannot use a subcomponent independently without the parent component. We can also abuse the term "physical" to describe distinct boundaries between different functions. For example, AWS and Google Cloud Platform (GCP) might be running on the same servers, but they are completely different company offerings. If they were running on the same servers, it would be very unlikely that you would know it. You can think of this as a physical boundary.

Multitenant

Currently, Salesforce instances are all hosted on Salesforce-owned/proprietary hosting systems. Each group of systems (instance) typically hosts many customers. Some customers are big enough or have enough special requirements that they are the sole customer on an instance. Everyone else shares and lives side-by-side with other customers. Data, compute, and memory are all managed by the application platform. The underlying platform has the ability to see any problems at the instance level and migrate customers to non-impacted systems when needed almost imperceptibly. Additionally, there are platform rules that keep one customer from affecting another that shares the same resources. Tools like Salesforce that are said to be "born in the cloud" are characterized by an elite level of availability, scalability, and security segmentation.

Oracle

The actual backend database for Salesforce is currently an Oracle implementation. This is informational only, because it is many layers deep in the logical stack beneath what users, admins, and even developers will ever see. It's actually something of a badge of honor if you manage to create a problem so novel that it generates an error condition that passes through an unhandled error that shows its pedigree all the way to Oracle.

The Salesforce platform has several data access interfaces that are logically similar to those found in classical databases, but it's important to know that they are layers upon layers. For the most part, you should never have to worry about the actual nature of the "metal" or the database; the interfaces are sufficiently surfaced for all scalable and performance-friendly needs. Interfaces or consumable resources that risk impact to multitenant shared resources either are not surfaced or are very highly governed (governor limits are discussed in the following section).

Hyperforce (the Future of the "Metal")

The base Salesforce server stack and metal (those two terms are blurry due to the buried nature of the physical layers in the PaaS/SaaS offerings) has been proprietary until recently. Salesforce maintains its own server farms with limited geographic redundancy. A visit to the Salesforce Status site (*https://status.salesforce.com*) can yield an understanding of how the physical resources are currently distributed (hosting, a.k.a. colocation).

Hyperforce is a new infrastructure architecture that allows the conversion/migration of Salesforce hosting to AWS hosting. This gives customers the ability to license Salesforce configured with additional options to meet their higher availability and fault tolerance requirements. This migration also enables redundant server pairs and availability zones. There was once a talk of allowing customers to choose the option of hosting on GCP or Azure as an alternative, but that seems to have evaporated; some organizations have a strong preference for one or the other, but currently there is only one option. While other hosting providers, like Microsoft, still have a physical-centric (or at least adjacent) provisioning model that you can attach a server mentality to, Salesforce and AWS do not. Salesforce's resource concepts are almost exclusively based on resource consumption and licenses.

Since multitenant resource management is moving from Salesforce's metal to AWS cloud provisioning, will the governor limits concept change? Presumably, AWS workload management might have more flexibility to allow advanced functionality and relaxation of governor limits. It would likely require a huge fork in the functionality of the Salesforce platform to option governor limits per org, though, so this will at least be significantly further out on the roadmap, if it happens at all. Tight governor limits give Salesforce the ability to predict *its* usage of AWS resources, and thus its costs. So, this may not be something that is public, but it might be discreetly possible at some point.

Enterprise Architecture Capabilities

This will not be a popular set of diagrams, as most people do not see Salesforce this way. However, this is the lure of Salesforce that is foiled by its name. The Salesforce ecosystem is on par with the other mega-giant cloud powerhouses out there. In the same way that Microsoft is no longer about microcomputer software and Amazon is neither about the rainforest nor selling books, Salesforce is not about sales or even CRM anymore.

There are many undermarketed, big-picture capabilities available in the Salesforce ecosystem that are overshadowed by its name, and the popularity of its namesake functionality. Salesforce overlaps both Microsoft and Amazon (and other big players in the space, like Oracle and IBM) in terms of enterprise functionality. This section cherry-picks a few examples of recent acquisitions and developments that demonstrate this, for the purposes of illustration. This isn't an exhaustive list; the point is to be aware of the complete range of in-platform or platform-adjacent capabilities so that you know when it's cheaper or more efficient to enable versus integrate. For example, you may already own a business intelligence (BI) system, but shuttling Salesforce data to it may be more costly than using Salesforce's built-in BI/ reporting capabilities.

Trying to establish component definitions in the era of modern cloud services is an exercise in futility. The following definitions will try to draw the Platonic ideal of a concept like a "knife" or a "screwdriver," but today almost every offering is a Swiss Army knife chimera. Some products, like Kafka, are now almost synonymous with their functions, like Kleenex. Please be wary of terms that have potential contextual changes.

PaaS

Heroku is a PaaS offering that allows hosting and dynamic allocation with pricing based on a pay-as-you-go consumption model. It's popular for mobile app hosting, data crunching, large data storage, and more. Heroku is a relatively recent acquisition. With it, Salesforce now has its own cloud (using the classic definition).

Heroku is a licensing and management skin-frastructure built on top of AWS, so to say it competes with the AWS cloud is imprecise. It does bring many AWS/Azure-esque abilities under the Salesforce umbrella, but few of these abilities offer much in the way of benefit to Salesforce over other third-party offerings.

Integration Platform as a Service (IPaaS)

MuleSoft is another recent acquisition that signaled titan-level maturity. Most people think of Salesforce as a silo platform that occasionally connects to other systems, but the inclusion of MuleSoft showed just how important integrations and data centralization have become in the ecosystem.

MuleSoft might be more accurately called an "API orchestration as a service" offering, due to some missing or nascent features that are common in other IPaaS solutions that you might be more familiar with.

Business Intelligence

Tableau was already established as a major player in the BI and reporting space when Salesforce acquired it. It maintains popularity among data scientists and reporting experts, as well as creating a maturity path from in-application reporting tools into a world-class BI framework.

In addition, Salesforce is one of the many platforms that has invested heavily in Snowflake's offerings (Snowflake is a cloud-based data warehouse service that contains a combination of data storage and data sharing tools; it's becoming a very common choice for providing data to reporting systems like Tableau). Salesforce-specific integration features regularly drop from Snowflake, showing that while it is not a Salesforce property, it is very clearly central in Salesforce's data actualization pathway.

Documents and Collaboration

Quip is a web-based document management system. Another fairly recent acquisition, it adds document creation, collaboration, management, storage, and integration capabilities to the core Salesforce platform. Quip is quietly a functional competitor to Microsoft Office Online, SharePoint, and OneDrive, as well as offering identical functions to Google Docs and Google Drive.

Collaboration and Chat

In 2021 Salesforce acquired Slack, a chat-centric collaboration system that gained fame with its integrations to major development systems like Git and Jira. Slack has exploded in popularity over the past few years, thanks to its support for inline and streamlined developer communications. Its key features have been imitated by many of the prior leaders in the space. Zoom and Microsoft Teams are now in constant feature competition, though Teams has the lion's share of users (this current market advantage is likely due to its bundling with Windows and Office licensing).

BPM, RPA, and Low-Code

Visual Flows, MuleSoft, and OmniScripts all have flavors of low-code, visual design, robotic process automation (RPA), and business process management (BPM) tools. Citizen developers can quickly get up to speed with these always-growing development systems, but they aren't perfect and can lead to confusion with so many options as in-platform peers. Nevertheless, they do seem to be the way of the future, as the popularity of low-code tools continues to grow.

Application Development

The Salesforce core platform supports a variety of automation and customization frameworks that range from proprietary to industry standard. Apex, the primary language in Salesforce, is very similar to Java in syntax. It seems to be a very mature and extensible specification, but it's only one of the languages in use in different capacities in the Salesforce ecosystem. This means that there are limits to how much you can do with it, and how often you can do it. Generally these don't pose a problem for small companies, and large companies have alternatives galore. Medium-sized companies, however, may face challenges due to growing pains and lack of affordable self-sponsored options. There are many consumption-based, third-party providers they can farm work out to, but this can quickly lead to complexity in systems and licensing, and a growth plan is essential.

Extensible Headless Compute (Lambdas)

Salesforce Functions is a new, independently licensed Lambda compute functionality that lets in-platform Apex code that is governed by multitenant rules and governor limits call out to an AWS-based compute stack. It removes the barrier of compute limitations, allowing you to perform large I/O and compute operations externally and return results or data to the platform. You are also not limited to writing code in Apex, as Salesforce Functions allows running of Java, TypeScript, and JavaScript. This opens up a new world of open source projects written in those languages that can be easily harnessed to quickly launch complicated functions (no need to reinvent the wheel in Apex). Salesforce Functions hasn't seen much public adoption, however, and it has a questionable path forward. Fortunately, there are ways to accomplish the same things in Heroku or with traditional AWS Lambdas.

Enterprise Software Capabilities

Salesforce is an application built to be a platform for others to build applications on. As such, it offers a variety of platforms, components, features, and applications for enterprise use. Whereas you used to have to buy, install, set up, and provide power for all of these yourself (or pay someone else to), now there is a web interface that abstracts these originally physical jobs into a few clicks, with the same results.

Table 2-1 gives some examples, in a few hypothetical contexts; the following subsections dig into the terminology.

Table 2-1. Term examples

	University enrollment	Water plant maintenance	Lemonade stand
Platform	Salesforce	Salesforce, MuleSoft	Salesforce, Marketing Cloud
Components	Apex, Flows	Apex, Lightning Web Components	Apex, Interaction Studio
Features	Sales Cloud, Service Cloud, Experience Cloud	Field Service Lightning, Service Cloud, custom indexes	Sales Cloud, CDC Plus, high-volume platform events
Applications	University of Internet Student Blazer Portal	EGPower Inspector	Nextgen Drink Sales and Marketing

Platforms

A *platform* is a surface or framework for building functionality. There can be platforms at many tiers or conceptual layers of the internet, but for most of our purposes we will be focused on PaaS frameworks for delivering web functionality. Salesforce the company owns several platform service providers. Salesforce the platform is a platform (duh). Many of the components within the Salesforce platform could also be considered platforms. Think of this as the foundation of a house. A second-story foundation could be built on top of the first foundation. Both are fairly clean slates upon which to assemble things. This is an engineering concept.

Components

A *component* is something built or reusable within any platform. Components are one of the many things that are created by engineers for reuse by themselves or other engineers. Components are the wood, nails, and concrete of a building. They are used to assemble and build features and applications. Components are generally available to all engineers on the platform as designed by the engineers that built them.

 The term component is also used in a slightly different context within Salesforce development, to refer to "packages" of code. (In Chapter 8, please see the discussions of Aura and Lightning Web Components.)

Features

Feature is another term with a lot of loose usage and overlap. For the purposes of this book, a feature is one or more components or pieces of functionality that is either enabled or not. Features can be turned on or off for use by end engineers. Features can provide end user functionality or engineering capabilities.

Applications

In this context, the term *application* refers to any grouping of functionality delivered to an end user. It is an assembly of components and features of a platform, possibly in conjunction with other platforms (integrations), to deliver a business process capability. An application is where the engineering components (and features) unite with the concepts of permissions, users, and business or application processes. Everything you build on Salesforce or connect to Salesforce could meet the definition of a single application, or you could surface many groupings of functionality and call them all applications. The meaning of the term is very arbitrary in general conversation. The Employee Portal application could just provide links to other applications on other platforms, but the end user might only be aware of the Portal as the application they use. All the participant systems/applications might also be managed collectively by the same group of people and referred to collectively as "the Portal."

The spectrum of definitions for an application can be as broad as "any perceived unification of functionality under any single perspective." (AWS is one application because you manage it from a single website.) It could also be as narrow as "a few lines of code." (I wrote an application in Excel to help me update cells.) See Table 2-1 for some example standard usages of the macro concept of applications.

If a platform, feature, or component provides no utility to a business user, then it is *not* an application (again, only for most of the purposes of this book).

 Salesforce has more than a few specific uses for the term *application*. Multiple applications (tabs) could be part of an application in this definition.

Why this definition? As an enterprise architect, most of my application value mapping examinations have been trying to measure the value and cost of running systems. Value is most easily mapped to the benefit derived from a unit of a system that provides a distinct business function. Comparative value mapping requires having some concept that can translate from system to system and platform to platform. There are many application lifecycle management (ALM) tools that you can use to map various costs and concepts, but that requires investment and discipline. The cheap and cheerful route that many companies opt for is to do this "by department." In the modern cloud era, however, this approach is very limiting and leads to IT silos. Transitioning to functional granularity requires a lot of blended organizational cooperation. Highly cooperative and transparent organizational practices yield the most accelerated and innovative businesses. Trying to achieve this goal means being able to address everything in units of value. Then you must leave as few nebulous shared-resource monoliths as possible in place. Working on a shared platform can make that really hard, but the effort can make all the difference in a capability-driven organization. The alternative is that the department that has the biggest budget makes all the decisions, regardless of the fit or total value proposition. These are extremes; choose your position on the spectrum wisely.

Functional Capabilities and Products

For awareness, this section presents a list of business functions that have a decent amount of maturity as product lines within Salesforce. This is not intended to be comprehensive. Using the definition of "application" from the previous section, there are quite a few features of the native platform that are *almost* usable out of the box by end users and could be standalone functions. Most of the functions require data and configuration to have functional value to an end user. Suppose, for example, that you are enabling a Sales organization with Sales Cloud on the Salesforce platform. Users cannot use it until someone has:

- Created user identities for accessing the tool
- Created a permission structure for who can see what
- Set up the number of steps in your sales process
- Added or loaded your existing customer base
- Trained users on how to appropriately load customers and contacts
- Explored the processes that are supposed to happen when users do things in the system (there are only a few actions that happen automatically without being configured to do so by default)
- Defined the way users and data will be stored in the primary data structures

Since the Sales Cloud feature needs to be configured and populated with business functional rules and operational data, it is not able to deliver business functionality.

The discussion of products will be limited due to the fact that most of the product branding and licensing line items have little bearing on infrastructure or architectural concepts. Some of the architecture features are licensed; some are seamless. There are products for:

- Customer relationship management
- Industry-specific functions like:
  — Health
  — Commerce
  — Banking
  — Sales
  — Ordering
  — Billing
- Marketing
- Collaboration
- Office utilities

A lot of these product offerings are either features or mini-platforms, without a good rule for determining which is which. This book won't say much about the business process capability offerings inside of Salesforce's functional offerings, unless they cross an important technical boundary. You can easily find documentation on the things you can buy on the Salesforce website (*https://www.salesforce.com*); we will continue to focus on what you need to know to manage, secure, connect, and implement Salesforce core functional offerings with other clouds or platforms.

 You can find a list of products and pricing information on the Salesforce Product Pricing page (*https://oreil.ly/782LL*).

Summary

While more traditional cloud offerings from other vendors have more direct "X license equates to your usage of Y physical resource" relationships, in Salesforce the lines can seem blurry. With Microsoft you're mostly paying for systems like SQL Server, Exchange Server, or desktop applications such as Excel; with AWS you're paying for compute or storage. Salesforce is more licensed by functionality. You're paying for features. Some of those features have distinct containers, but focus on the functional. Some products are loosely coupled to stacks using other stacks, and some features will just be licensing to change a soft limit of the number of widget operations you can do in a 24-hour period (like rollover minutes). Products may be called "applications" or "features" but include changes to the metal and touch everything in between.

Although it can seem like you are trying to understand an Escher-esque licensing model, the goal is to make the consumption model as granular as possible so that customers only pay for what they need. Bundles are available too. I will be calling out some boundaries that only have a relationship to licensing (e.g., governor limits), but won't spend much time on them since they are mostly code-level and performance management minutiae. Please refer back to these first two chapters for term reference and boundary definitions often as you progress.

CHAPTER 3

Platform Data Concepts

As architects, we need to understand the shape of data models and the ways to interact with them. Successful enterprise systems work by maximizing efficiencies and minimizing resistance. Resistance can be defined as the opposite of ease: anything that requires extra effort or resources to maintain creates resistance.

Each platform does different things in different ways. When creating solutions with different platforms, it's important to understand how easily their data models can be shared or work together. For example, Salesforce can process updates to single data records quickly and easily. If you need to work with other systems that can also perform fast and easy single data record updates, those systems can be expected to work together with little resistance.

On the other hand, relative to other systems, Salesforce is not as fast at updates that involve large numbers of data records. If you want to integrate with a system that can natively handle large record transfers or updates much faster than Salesforce, you have resistance. You might need to add an intermediary system, like a high-performance data store. Alternatively, you could build a custom inbound or outbound processing component to manage the extra time required to complete the operation. This additional infrastructure or code is the resistance. Another example is dealing with complex or deep hierarchies. Salesforce has only limited support for displaying relationships that require complex joins with other objects. It's a fairly common workaround within Salesforce, especially for report building, to flatten data to support reporting requirements. Hierarchical data is copied to individual records so that reports can be built and include relationships with other objects. Other systems don't have this quirk/limitation and may store hierarchies in a completely different way. Sharing hierarchies between systems with different quirks can require more work. This is another form of resistance.

Architects design solutions anticipating resistance and leveraging efficiencies. As Salesforce builds and acquires more functionality that better supports scale, part of your job will be identifying the "tipping point" where a smaller/cheaper/simpler solution is no longer a good fit.

We'll begin this chapter by discussing the most important Salesforce data concepts at the row level, then work our way up to the more conceptual I/O and pattern levels. We'll also go over the implications of all of Salesforce's (the application) data being accessible only via web service APIs. After we talk about how data is organized inside Salesforce, we'll move on to external relationships and data sources.

Basic Technical Architecture of an RDBMS

The following concepts and components are common to many relational database management systems (RDBMSs). While some of them are not exposed for users or developers to interact with, they still play a role, and it's important to understand how they might relate to other systems you are working with:

Listener
> The listener is the system process that is called by remote systems that receives requests for data. This is where service account credentials are processed. (This is at the system level; when data is published to a web service, other logical layers may be involved.)

Query optimizer
> The query optimizer parses a query and forms the "plan" for how to retrieve the requested data. You can work with the query optimizer inside the Salesforce Developer Console, adjacent to the query builder.

Joins and sorts
> The database system contains a variety of internal mechanisms to manage and streamline the work involved in sorting and joining data for output. These can vary within a system as well as having many differences from other types of databases.

Indexes
> A simple way to create an index is by converting a field or column of data that is often part of an alphabetical ordering request into numbers. It's much easier for the query optimizer to order (sort) things by these numbers than it would be to sort them alphabetically. Remember, this sorting happens every time the data is requested. To make requests fast, indexes are usually updated whenever data is loaded or changed (i.e., on *writes*) so that it is always available when a *read* happens. This adds "work" to the write processes to make the read processes faster.

Views

A view is a reduced section of a table or joined tables that's defined by a query. Using views can improve performance, since the query optimizer has already figured out how to perform the data operations when the view is created.

Materialized views

When a view is "materialized," not only is the structure of the query stored, but the data is also stored for a period of time. If a complicated query is performed often and the underlying data doesn't change frequently, it can be very efficient to reuse the results for a period of time without refreshing them from the "real" data. *Skinny tables* in Salesforce are somewhere between views and materialized views. You can't create, access, or modify skinny tables yourself; you have to ask your account team to set them up.

Triggers

Triggers are code or scripts in a database that are run either when called or upon some event, such as a data change. Triggers can be used to listen for many types of events and perform some action before or after the event occurs. This is the most often used term for automation driven by a database change event within Salesforce. Stored procedures are not used in Salesforce.

Data

Data in databases can be stored or processed in many different ways. It's commonly visualized as a collection of columns and rows stored in files on a hard drive somewhere, but modern databases can store data in a variety of formats and memory structures, in files with multiple layers and nesting. A cell in a database table might contain a zero, a name, a date, or an XML structure with gigabytes of nested names, dates, and other data. You don't always need to know the details of the data structure inside your database system, but understanding the work it has to do to maintain the data will help you build and maintain efficient applications.

Figure 3-1 shows how these components fit together in a typical RDBMS. Data queries (also called *reads* or *selects*) come in at the top and make their way to the bottom. Salesforce has a layer of software on top of these components, but when working with the software you will benefit from knowing what's behind it. One of the many "secret sauces" of Salesforce is that the software provides most of the native functions (with added security and scalability to multiple customers) baked in.

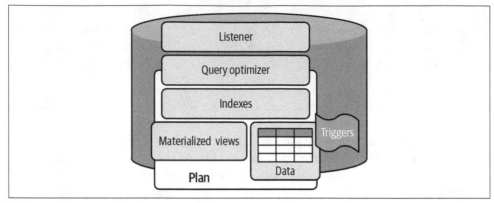

Figure 3-1. A generic RDBMS model

Tables and Rows

There are several vocabulary items to absorb here. Salesforce has its own terms for rows and columns of data: tables are *objects*, rows are *records*, columns are *fields*. These are fairly normal variants of data container vocabulary. The terms used specifically for data manipulation language concepts can get more confusing when you combine the programming language corollaries for data types and structures. We won't be focusing much on those in this chapter on data.

The more challenging concepts have to do with how the platform has imposed a "liberating restriction" on how relationships can be established. It's a simplification of the type of relationships that are possible in other database systems. These differences can be hard to acclimate to for those with experience in SQL and data development. The restrictions lead to a simplicity of design choices that can make maintenance and discovery very simple.

Logic and validation are also very tightly connected to the data. All data access is passing through the application logic layer so things that are normally only relevant in the display/UI layer are active when you are accessing data. There is no direct "SQL" level access to the data even with the SOQL access points. (SOQL is an SQL variant that can be used to query Salesforce data.) Requests for data are still going through a filter of a filter of a filter. This is not an uncommon practice with multitenant or SaaS platforms. It does mean that you may need to adjust your models as you deal with Salesforce data. In other words, you may not be able to bulk import records due to a restriction that, in other systems, exists for users during application page interactions.

There are two main types of objects in Salesforce: standard objects and custom objects. (We'll look at a few other types later in this chapter.) *Standard objects* are central to a given piece of Salesforce functionality and are included by default. For example, common business objects like User, Contact, and Account are available with the core platform. Other objects, like Opportunity, are only included with the Sales Cloud functionality, but even though they aren't included in all instances, they are still called "standard." Standard objects can have extra logic or functions tied to them. Screens, relationships, and triggers can also come packaged with standard objects. You can add additional fields and functionality to standard objects, but it's not a great idea to remove functions from them, as doing so can have unintended consequences.

Custom objects are objects that you create yourself. You can name and build fields and relationships for these objects however you want, within some constraints (there are a handful of protected words and special character considerations to be aware of). Depending on the settings that you configure as you create them, other objects may be created at the same time behind the scenes. For example, creating a Track Field History object will cause an additional History object to be created automatically.

All objects are created with several default pieces of functionality that take a lot of work out of the traditional schema definition process. All records are automatically given an encoded identity field. The ID field is structured and contains data that can tell you what object and organization the record belongs to. Creation and modification times are kept for every record, along with the UserID of the user who created/modified the record. Change tracking can also be configured easily on any object. Deleted records can be retrieved from the Recycle Bin if needed.

Since almost all of the ecosystem's configuration is exposed or accessible via APIs, all of the data about your configuration is referred to as *metadata*. You can take this as shorthand for all the config data in Salesforce. However, the term can also refer to actual user data. Additionally, Salesforce has an internal object structure called Custom Metadata (CMDT) that is more of a dimensional table structure, as opposed to relational data in the database. There are also layers of in-memory data that exist more as cache data. We won't be covering caching in this book.

Relationships

Salesforce allows you to start creating usable applications without defining a data model, but many tenured application architects struggle with the common practice of putting the user interface before the data relationships. Before building any system, application architects will build an *entity relationship diagram* (ERD) like the one shown in Figure 3-2.

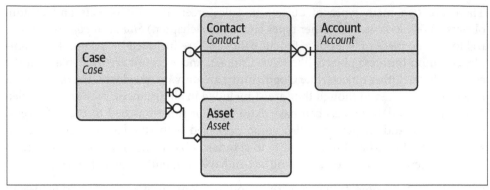

Figure 3-2. An example of an ERD

Database performance is heavily tied to an efficient data model, regardless of how many extra safety features are added on top of the data layer. Salesforce has a Schema Builder tool to help visualize data relationships, but I find that it is not used or reviewed enough. Lack of data model management and relationship rationalization can lead to relationship sprawl and poor performance.

Relationships are constrained to four effective types. We won't go into much detail, but you should know the terms. The implementations in Salesforce are nuanced, but these are the basics (taking some liberties for conceptual reasons):

Lookup
    When an object record has a pointer to another record in the same object or another object.

Parent–child
    Like a lookup, but the child has a tighter relationship with the parent and can inherit certain permissions from it. Enabling the inheritance of attributes like permissions is a further configuration of the lookup relationship type.

Master–detail
    A tighter relationship still. A detail record cannot exist without the master record. Deleting the master deletes the details. Details have few rights of their own; they are dependent on the master object.

Junction
    This is a many-to-many relationship that requires its own object. The junction object is a detail of two master objects. It provides the linkage record between those two objects.

There are other types of relationships with different objects and concepts, but you will have to work with these for most of your in-platform data.

RecordTypes

To maintain the simplicity of the data model, using RecordTypes is encouraged. A *RecordType* is an addressable collection of fields, rules, and records within an object (Figure 3-3). *Addressable* means that you can assign fields, screens, rules, and specifics within the object's fields and definitions. RecordTypes connect the individual records to all of these other features. An object can have no or many RecordTypes (for example, an Account object might have Customer and Partner RecordTypes defined). Behind the scenes, a RecordType is a field on the object that points to the RecordType object as a lookup. You can lead your users to create specific Record-Types per your application process. You should use RecordTypes any time that a logical concept overlaps with an existing logical concept or object. Drop-down fields can have different values based on their RecordType. They give you most of the abilities of a separate object while keeping the data model simple.

 Core internal data terminology can be confusing. Salesforce grew up as a salesperson's best friend. In Salesforce, the term *account* means *customer* and most often refers to the company that a salesperson is selling to. A *contact* is a person that works for the account (company) that a salesperson interacts with or keeps records on. A *user* is a person that logs into Salesforce. The user has a username and user record in Salesforce and keeps track of contacts with their sales target accounts. In other systems, an "account" is synonymous with a login identity or user account.

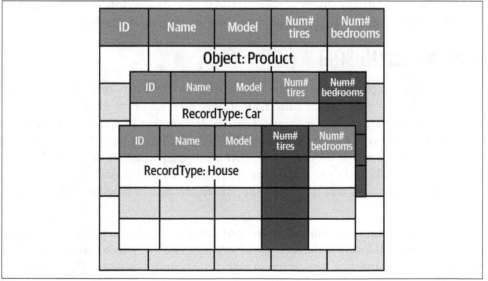

Figure 3-3. RecordType visualization

Triggers and Flows

Triggers have long been the core of the Salesforce custom functionality capability, to the point where programming in Salesforce is generally taken to mean writing triggers. Triggers are written in the Apex language (*https://oreil.ly/RAHdu*), which is a Java-esque, object-oriented, just-in-time pseudo-language. They're their own type of Apex code, and they can call other classes that are also Apex code. It's common for the processing performed by a trigger to be contained in a separate class that it calls, known as a helper class, as this makes it easier to reuse the trigger for other purposes. Other functions besides triggers are written in Apex (see Chapter 8), but the trigger is the main layer of data flow control.

Flows are another customization and automation layer that allow you to control the flow of data within Salesforce. Flows are built within a visual environment and can also call Apex classes.

Workflow Rules and Process Builder are two sunsetting automation layers that are invoked upon data change. These are both on a scheduled deprecation path, so you should not be creating new functions with them. Already existing workflows and processes will continue to function for some time, however, so you should be aware of these terms. We'll talk more about all three of these in Chapter 8.

From a Salesforce perspective, all of the automation layers are executed as equal partners with an established, well-documented order of execution. In other ecosystems, SQL and triggers execute very close to the database layer. This is several layers away from the application logic, where flows and other data logic live. Triggers are usually only written by database administrators (DBAs) or data developers. Application or business logic/code is written by a different team of application developers.

Big Objects (NoSQL)

Big objects have recently been added to the platform's data ecosystem. Big objects are recommended for data storage patterns that have high numbers of records but little actual daily use (high write, low read). Forensic transaction logs and change history tracking are the most common candidates for big objects. The limitations around big objects strongly hint that they are an in-platform implementation of a NoSQL structure, similar to MongoDB or Cassandra. They can be queried, but not in the same way as normal objects, and they don't support as many field type options as regular objects.

Big objects allow for almost infinite storage of data produced within Salesforce. However, there are still limits to the amount of data you can bring into Salesforce, so this isn't (currently) a practical option for an enterprise object/data store. There are some hacks that can be used to get Salesforce to work with really large sets of records, but big objects are capable of handling orders of magnitude more. I'm hoping to see them mature and scale to find more frequent use as an application component in the future. For the time being, if you are working with large datasets that need to be actively consumed or sent to other systems, you'll have to choose another system.

External Objects (Mapped Data Sync) and Files

External objects in Salesforce are a very useful way of interacting with large sets of external data without having to build a bespoke synchronization pattern. An external object consists of an internal object that keeps an external primary key as a pointer to an outside record. Making this connection is effectively mapping the external data as if it were an internal object. There are licensing- and connection-based concerns, but this is one of the best ways to get external data available to the native functions of the platform.

There are limits to the number of external objects you can create, and other limits regarding the number of outbound connections that can affect when and how you implement them. External objects can also include mappings to unstructured files like documents and images. Working with mapped objects has many benefits, but can be quite chatty from an I/O perspective. Make sure you are managing your complexity and connectivity to keep highly connected objects from being a potential point of failure. This is also called *data virtualization*.

Remote Data Queries

The next best method to access external data is via remote queries. Salesforce supports synchronous and asynchronous web service calls that can pass queries to remote systems and receive data back and process it. The returned data can be loaded into objects or be exposed directly to a user. The biggest downside is that external data changes don't launch flows or trigger automation in Salesforce like internal object changes do. So, using remote data queries and storage needs to be weighed against the real-time and reactive capabilities you are building. This is the difference between reference data and data that drives the interaction and value stream you are building.

Any large implementation benefits greatly from doing a data valuation and segmentation exercise prior to dreaming up the functional landscape. As for cheap structured data storage, the most adjacent product to use is Heroku (Salesforce's infrastructure as a service option). Heroku's platform is regularly used to house a PostgreSQL instance. Heroku also gives you the ability to host other finely tuned data provider systems, like Redshift, BigQuery, Kafka, NoSQL variants, and Elasticsearch.

Flat File Data

Salesforce supports some flat file imports, but only at very small scales (~50k records). For anything larger or automated, you will be using external tools to break the files into chunks that can be pushed into Salesforce with a series of API calls. Data Loader is a Java-based local/server application that can map and push large sets of data to Salesforce. This is very often installed on an on-premises server and run on a schedule. While this can be a sustainable practice for organizations with a heavy file-based infrastructure, many opt to offload this task to a third-party data service. Mule-Soft is an easy option that is owned by Salesforce, but there are many third-party vendors that work in this space as service providers or add-ins. There are easy integration patterns that allow you to upload new or synchronize existing data. These patterns require identifying remote system foreign keys, after which the imports can route the data as "new" or "updates." There are also many third-party services that can process flat files and turn them into web service updates.

 Many Salesforce practitioners are familiar with these components, which are either owned by Salesforce or one degree of Kevin Bacon from the core offerings. It's important to understand the architectures being proposed for your organization. You may already have a powerful middleware or extract, transform, load (ETL) system, but the incoming team may not have experience with it or appreciate the roles certain elements are supposed to play. Good architects parachute into solution discussions early and share key functional capabilities before designs get built with expensive duplication.

The Good

The data layer of the Salesforce platform has a lot in common with other platform application tools. Salesforce has baked in a considerable amount of security on top of the data components that make building serious applications feasible with high security in mind. The data features feel complete for building functionality. Once you have a good grasp of the fundamentals, you can accomplish what you need to get done. There is a lovely data model visualization tool called Schema Builder built into Salesforce, but it's chronically underused and unfortunately it cannot be used as a standalone enterprise component due to limitations that favor internal usage. The schema should be built first for any solution and communicated out to the people who will be building the automation or pages. Functionality should be designed around relationships and rules, not the other way around. Hopefully, more tools that can export and annotate data models will continue to evolve.

The Gotchas

Protecting the shared data resources for a multitenant platform does involve sacrificing some functionality. Salesforce deliberately firewalls off capabilities that could reduce shared resource availability. Enabling bulk loading of data and working with unstructured data storage (files) is one of the first third-party investments that large projects often make. Total data storage in Salesforce (data + files/attachments) is counted toward a separate licensing cost. Storing too much data inside Salesforce can quickly become expensive, so it's very common to leverage Amazon S3 for document storage requirements.

Working with flat files or data extracts is another area where Salesforce has a bit of a gap, but there are plenty of options from third parties to handle these as needed. I think the best practice that Salesforce is trying to de facto enforce is that everything should be web service to web service. There are a few in-platform methods for importing comma-separated values (CSV) files, but they have their limits. Architects managing ecosystems that are heavily reliant on data files for syncing and sharing will need to consider this additional effort.

The Growth

Improved data functionality and capabilities seems to be a major focus of the development team. Subtle changes that provide order-of-magnitude gains in data capability show up regularly. Many of these updates don't get the proper fanfare they deserve, based on the scale of the improvements they enable. Much of the real growth around the concept of data models is creating access to systems that hold bigger data models and allow easier integration. Big objects, Genie (discussed in Chapter 5), Tableau, and MuleSoft are all game-changing avenues for scaling and maturing your applications.

Summary

The Salesforce data fabric as a whole contains a lot of capabilities that align with those of traditional enterprise data platforms. You can achieve full parity with what other cloud hosting providers offer, but it requires a concerted effort and coordination of multiple product lines. This is to say that you shouldn't expect to be able to easily migrate a large data center into Salesforce as is. At smaller scales, there is absolutely a representative component for everything you could conceivably need to run your business. To me, this is the biggest winning proposition of Salesforce: you need a top-tier selling tool, and the Salesforce ecosystem has at least good options for every other function you might require. Other platform providers may have some pieces of the puzzle as well, but not all of them.

You can start a business in Salesforce. You can grow and thrive in Salesforce. However, as soon as you get to the point where you are running large-scale anything, you will need to plan your approach carefully. In the next chapter we will delve into more of the hurdles that you might face when trying to use different components together to make solutions that push the boundaries beyond simple use cases.

CHAPTER 4

Data and Architecture Constraints

In this chapter we will dive deeper into the enterprise fit of the Salesforce architecture components. Some of the players in this space are open source offerings, some are third-party, and several are now owned by Salesforce. The products and companies discussed here should be taken as examples of the archetypes and not as recommendations. There are many valid options in each of these product industries. The important thing is to be aware of when scale factors might lead you to choose additional products outside of the Salesforce platform. Take another look at Figure 2-3 to review the basic definitions of resource types that are sold, provisioned, and used in a cloud service offering. The management of these resources will strongly influence your architecture. Figure 4-1 shows some of the areas that Salesforce architects expand into. In this chapter we will explore some of the reasons behind such expansions.

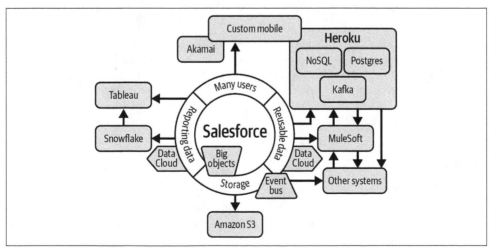

Figure 4-1. Large-scale data patterns

Complexity Boundaries

Working in Salesforce requires limiting the complexity of your data structures. Complex structures can have severe impacts on performance in any system. Salesforce has implemented many restrictions and limits to prevent unhealthy patterns. For example, if you have ever worked to tune query performance by avoiding full table scans and table locking, the best practices will be familiar to you. You will just be using new tools to manage joins, locking, indexing, and other query optimizations. With these restrictions in place, working in Salesforce means that you don't always have the luxury of starting out with loose disciplines and later implementing more performant strategies.

Data skew (*https://oreil.ly/BUxyu*) is a concern brought about by the automatic referential integrity enforcement of certain Salesforce data concepts. In very broad terms, if one record has a relationship to several thousand other records, making changes to that record can cause locks. This is a one-sentence definition of a very deep database management concept. The numbers vary, and the actual impact can be small or large depending on the application. The point is that improperly estimating and planning for how your data relationships will scale can lead to a lot of rework. The orders of magnitude are what you want to be aware of, so that you can design around them.

Salesforce Object Query Language (SOQL), the platform's data access language, has a lot of time-saving shortcuts built into it. It's actually quite handy once you get used to it. If you have a background in other flavors of SQL, this is a good way to repurpose your existing knowledge. SOQL (or, more accurately, the Salesforce data access APIs) does have a few limitations that require knowledge to navigate, though. For example, you can build queries that reference relationships up to five levels deep, but no further. The built-in reporting functions also have limitations related to data complexity.

 It is a very common, albeit cringe-inducing, practice to write codelets that flatten (denormalize) data to get around complexity boundaries. Small and medium organizations don't usually have a problem with the I/O penalty of such hacks, but a larger implementation would want to plan for storing larger hierarchies in more appropriate systems.

Size Boundaries

Storage is another coveted resource that is governed heavily within the core Salesforce ecosystem. It aims to be an agile user interface and data processing layer, and heavy storage exacts a toll on resources that Salesforce prefers to keep in check. Any attachments or files are usually better kept in a more tuned tier. Salesforce can also present challenges in dealing with binary large object (BLOB) data types (things that would consume memory while processing).

Salesforce has a few options for dealing with file storage and access that are fairly easy to implement. Amazon S3 is a common choice for storing files that are either large or need to be available long term. Other common candidates include Google Drive, OneDrive, and SharePoint. Many offer seamless plug-ins to connect your data needs and processes with your remotely stored files.

Compute Boundaries

A *transaction* in Salesforce is the cumulative set of processes and CPU time associated with any specific user or automated starting point. If a user clicks a button that starts a workflow that creates a record that has a trigger that calls a web service, and the data from that web service's response is written to another object that has another trigger that does some other things, all of that is a single transaction. Behind the scenes, each of these events is participating in a notification and timing framework that reports up to the governor system. If a transaction runs for longer than a specified threshold, the governor can stop it and force it to fail. At that time, many of the completed events from the prior parts of the transaction can be rolled back. The time limit for a synchronous transaction is 10 seconds. If you mix in asynchronous techniques, this can go up to 60 seconds.

I/O Boundaries

In this context, I'm using the term input/output (I/O) to refer to inbound and outbound calls to and from the Salesforce system. In general, outbound calls from Salesforce are not metered by the number of calls or the data returned. Inbound calls reading or pushing data into Salesforce are metered. The limits imposed are related to your licensing. Paying for additional features or more licensed users can grant you more headroom. The limits are soft limits and are in the multiples of millions per 24-hour period. You don't get cut off at your million-and-first inbound call, but you may get a call from your account representative to talk about increasing your spend if it happens regularly, and large excesses can lead to a large bill. This is probably the least of the boundaries that you will need to worry about, but it is there.

Object Polymorphism (Reusing Objects)

Best practices in Salesforce (for the sake simplicity and backend performance management) encourage *polymorphism* in objects. This is the practice of reusing database tables (objects) if their purpose is similar (i.e., if the objects would share a bunch of the same fields, like Name, Email, and Address). For example, you would not create a database table for Retail Customers and an additional one for Online Customers; you would use one table and create a flag field that tracked which type of customer each record represented. The mechanism used in Salesforce to accomplish this is called

RecordTypes (see Chapter 3). Establishing a new RecordType as an additional usage type of a database table brings a number of features for securing those types against other types. There are also data display options and other associated variations that can be provisioned to accessorize those new types as soon as they are created.

RecordTypes and polymorphism patterns create a lot of opportunity for reusability, but this comes at the price of dependencies. RecordTypes allow partitioning of some of the data features associated with an object, but not all of them. Field validation rules are created at the object level. They can be set to only restrict entries based on a specific RecordType, but they are still executed on every interaction of the object. This can pose a challenge for managing functionality across different teams of builders. We will cover this further in Chapter 12.

Built-in Advanced Database Functionality

Database tables that are created or exist by default have certain advanced database features automatically created for them. Experienced DBAs or data architects will be familiar with the concepts of primary keys, indexes, compound keys, and globally unique identifiers (GUIDs).

Every record in Salesforce is stamped with a unique identifier, stored in an ID field. This field is automatically created for each object that is available by default or that you create, and it is neither editable nor nullable. The ID field is populated automatically on record creation. The IDs are not completely random like standard GUIDs, though. While it may look random, a record's ID contains a lot of information. Incorporated in the ID are encoded (but not encrypted) references to the object that the record is an element of and the org/client that the record belongs to, as well as a Base64-encoded counter element. The first three characters are a reference to the object the record belongs to. For example, every record in the Account object has an ID that starts with 005. There are a lot of blog posts that go into detail on this on the internet; the key takeaway is that the IDs are not random, and if you know how to read them, they can contain important information.

 There are two variants of IDs that can be used or referenced with Salesforce records. First is the classic 15-character ID that can contain both upper- and lowercase letters and is case-sensitive. The newer 18-character version is not case-sensitive, and the extra characters account for this.

Indexes are much more important in Salesforce than many other systems. In other systems, indexes help improve the speed at which queries perform. In Salesforce, the lack of an index can determine whether a query will be run at all. Queries that are written for large tables without an appropriate index will return one of several "too many records" messages.

All foreign key (lookup) fields, including the Creator and Owner fields, are automatically indexed. RecordTypeID and system timestamp fields are also indexed by default. There are two ways to create indexes on your own (custom) fields: you can request one from customer support or add the External ID attribute to the field. Since indexed fields determine the ability to query objects with very large counts of records, managing and properly planning indexes can be critical to your system's operation.

When an object is created, several things happen in the background that are related to whether or how the object will be visible to end users. In many other systems, seeing a new object is not a given. In Salesforce, many of those Model, View, Controller distinctions are established at the same time. More classical systems completely separate the data structure from the data display. New pages are created automatically that include individual page layouts as well as list views for multiple records. It then becomes possible to assign permissions to the object and those pages. Depending on your security settings, creation of the object may automatically grant users access to the new pages or views, even if there are no records. Be aware of the potential to overshare data as these additional assets and references are created.

Geography

Related to compute and I/O challenges is the fact that until recently, Salesforce instances were hosted in region-specific data centers. If you are delivering highly customized experiences (e.g., graphics, multipage work processes, responsive experiences), you will want to consider your geography. If your users have high demands with regard to their connection to Salesforce, content delivery networks (CDNs) may need to play a role in your designs. CDNs can reduce the load on your Salesforce source and help users in distant regions have better experiences.

Geography can also play a role in your business continuity planning. With the advent of Hyperforce, as mentioned in Chapter 2, you now have cloud-scale options for where you have data redundancy in case of a regional disaster. Hyperforce was originally marketed as an option to have your Salesforce instance hosted on any of the major cloud platforms, like Google's GCP, Microsoft's Azure, or Amazon's AWS. This appealed to many businesses that were in competition with those companies, as it meant you'd be able to choose where to spend your hosting dollars. Unfortunately, that choice didn't materialize (or at least it hasn't yet). Currently, with Hyperforce all new Salesforce instances are transitioning from being hosted by Salesforce to being hosted in AWS. While not providing as much choice as originally advertised, this still brings some great options. For example, now when you are configuring your deployment, you can select availability zones for fault tolerance—if your organization requires that extra risk mitigation, it's now available.

There's some hope that moving to an AWS container model could lead to more personal control over all of the other limits discussed in this chapter. This is still speculation at this point, but it's nice to think that this level of customization and administration might be possible at some point.

Iterative Design

Agile development practices can lead to problems with Salesforce customization. All of the boundaries and ways that Salesforce was designed to work, as well as changes and additions to the product, should be constantly reviewed. Salesforce is a platform with many existing functional scaffolds that you should be working within. Iterative design can cause problems if the new iterations don't take into account the cumulative complexity and resource consumption of the final design. Resource contention and painting yourself into a corner are constant challenges, and you cannot just "throw hardware at it" in a hosted platform environment. Employing battle-scarred and #AlwaysLearning architects is the only way to build nontrivial applications without encountering nontrivial self-inflicted problems. It's much easier to redesign early with foresight than to attempt a redesign at the onset of a late-stage disaster. With the current market demand for architects to maintain and drive a successful vision, adding in many planning sessions and documentation is vital.

Master Data Management

Salesforce can consume and generate large amounts of both transactional and master data. Salesforce can also generate highly siloed teams. Developing a master data management (MDM) strategy for data that is used or resides within Salesforce is extremely important. This importance is not just operational or academic; it has a fiscal impact as well. Unmanaged growth of data can have real, tangible impacts on costs. It's very important to recruit and train data champions if your Salesforce implementation is going to create large numbers of records. Storage value versus storage cost should be constantly evaluated for any application, but managing resources in Salesforce can have a much more direct impact on cost than it does in some other platforms.

Reporting

Reporting can be casual or enterprise. Salesforce is very good at casual reporting, but if you are interested in deriving actual business insight from large amounts of data, you'll want to make use of a BI tool. Planning how and when to leverage Salesforce data for high-order reporting should be done early in the design phase. Salesforce has an internal report building system (Reports) that is great for basic reporting and provides some useful data sanity and review functions. It's able to produce good-looking, shareable reports, provided that your needs aren't too complex. It's possible to create more complex reports with the built-in reporting system too, but they can require adding some complexity-impacting relationships. This is due to the mechanics of the native reports being primarily based on real-time queries of the actual in-use data. More complex queries are only possible with data that is stored and processed separately from the internal live data. Cubes and other query flattening, caching, and pre-processing mechanisms are possible in Tableau and other modern BI and reporting tools. Look to these external systems if you have any serious data crunching requirements.

Speaking of serious data crunching, Tableau is one of the leading BI platforms worldwide, and it was recently acquired by the Salesforce corporation. Tableau is extremely mature and powerful; it can definitely handle any reporting requirements you have. It will be the most common suggestion from a Salesforce sales team (and using it will likely become more advantageous as it's further integrated into the Salesforce platform), but data is data and you should have no problem working with any other available modern BI platform.

Bulk Import of Data

The primary tool for bulk loading data from files (CSV) into Salesforce is called Data Loader. A client-based Java (OpenJDK) tool that runs on Windows or Mac, it can make use of bulk APIs to parse and load flat file-based data. Data Loader is a popular choice, in part because it's free. However, the web APIs for loading data are standard and usable by anything that can push HTTP and supports modern web authentication standards.

As this is one of the few server/local tools in the Salesforce ecosystem, be aware that security and virtualization boundaries can impact its use. Upload speeds can be affected by many variables, such as:

- Target object validations
- Target object relationship complexity
- Data structure of the file
- Network and virtual private network (VPN) speed
- Other tunnels and distance to Salesforce instance
- Server or virtual desktop infrastructure (VDI) memory, storage, and processor speed
- Data loss prevention (DLP) and other packet inspection overhead

There are two products called "Data Loader" that are part of Salesforce: Data Loader and dataloader.io. *Data Loader* is the downloadable Java application that Salesforce supports to do server- or PC-based batched data loads. This is the scriptable data import tool that is in wide use across the ecosystem. *dataloader.io* is part of the MuleSoft product line; it's an external web interface that allows loading of limited amounts of file data with no cost. dataloader.io is not to be confused with the File Import Wizard, an in-platform web interface included with Salesforce that also allows loading of small amounts of file data for no cost.

Most large enterprises should have some preferred version of a web-based middleware or ETL layer as their primary data feed system. Data Loader can be a very useful utility for loading test data or for initial loads prior to going live.

Another data access tool that is commonly used is Workbench. Workbench is a suite of free web-based tools that you can use to connect to your Salesforce instance and view and update your records. The use of Workbench is so prevalent that most people assume that it's part of the platform, but it's not actually owned by Salesforce; it's a website interface that lets you connect to a Salesforce instance. It is not recommended to use it for production data access. Workbench will let you query or bulk update records using data from a CSV file or manually. It is an extremely valuable tool for looking at data from a perspective not provided by the core interface.

The Good

With experience, you can implement just about every standard data pattern in Salesforce.

The Gotchas

Working with Salesforce data requires extra discipline. Data in Salesforce is only surfaced after the request passes through several layers of logic and permissions. It's also important to keep in mind that with Salesforce you're dealing with shared multitenant resources. Your data likely lives in the same database and same tables as that of many other customers. Legend has it that the actual database for each Salesforce pod has less than 20 tables. All other data structures are managed by filter logic. The net result of this is a maximum bandwidth or speed penalty. There are many governor systems watching your requests for data and I/O to make sure you are not going above certain limits that would negatively impact other users/customers. Batch processing, bulk loading, backups, and other workloads that could cause high CPU, I/O, or storage usage have to be specially structured to work within Salesforce. Storage of records as well as unstructured data (files) also comes at a premium.

Archiving strategies are not optional for use cases that involve rapid growth due to acquisitions. Changing data models is not an easily reversible scenario in Salesforce. Salesforce also doesn't include a specific backup and recovery solution. It is internally fault tolerant with redundancies, but many of these redundancies won't do you any good if you corrupt your own data by mistake.

Building a large-scale Salesforce implementation requires investment and management in multiple cloud technologies. Fortunately, it's fairly easy to grow into these additional systems over time. Cost and license management are their own disciplines. Make sure your growth plan includes regular reviews of sizing and cost.

Due to the limitations in types of relationships and data patterns, you are not always able to "lift and shift" existing applications into Salesforce. Very few development platforms have the same constraints around optimal-only relationships. You will have to closely examine the source data model for compatibility with Salesforce. Once you have a Salesforce-compatible data model, rebuilding functionality can be easy, but unless it is heavily based on JavaScript, it is unlikely to be quick. JavaScript can be easier to port (moving functionality built in one language or platform to another) than many other frameworks.

Data security management, with all of the layers that distributed data entails, must be a focus. This is another area that should be treated as its own discipline, and you should scale these efforts to the sensitivity and value of the data you are holding.

The Growth

While everything discussed in the previous section may sound intimidating, it's really just part of modern cloud architecture. The easiest way to explain how the different components work is by talking about at what point in the scaling process challenges arise. In the past few years, Salesforce has made many acquisitions that empower large-scale enterprise functions to be built in it and around it. Many of the gotchas are already starting to have bridges built over them.

The evolution of the platform event bus, which we'll look at in the next chapter, hints at a desire to allow data transfer within and out of the platform at a massive scale. The internals of the new bus are actually Kafka wrapped in some secret sauce enhancements. The Kafka high-volume streaming options are currently *inside-inside* or *inside-outside*, but that's likely to change as the offering ripens. The platform event bus promises to be a high-speed data conduit for future integrations, offloading data bus transfer resource consumption from the main platform.

Inside-inside refers to Salesforce platform components being able to publish and subscribe to events on the event bus at a very high scale. "Inside-outside" means that outside (external) systems can subscribe to the event bus at high volumes, though licensing dictates the maximum number of messages that can be received from the bus. There are also licensing limits on inbound publishing to the event bus from outside. The limits are high enough for some use cases, but depending on your needs, it's not likely to be cost-effective to use the event bus in place of a dedicated messaging service like Kafka.

Salesforce already had a respectable reporting framework before it bought Tableau. The Tableau acquisition should tell you that the company has goals beyond just "respectable." Acquiring tools like Tableau and Slack speaks to the motivation to have many features move from adequate to best-in-breed. Salesforce is also focusing on the world-class data enablement segment, with heavy investments in Snowflake. More and more seamless integrations with Snowflake turn up each day. Snowflake itself is evolving into much more than just an operational data store, to the point where it's actually a challenge to describe it with only a few key terms.

There are also constant enhancements being seen through Salesforce's partnership with AWS. Watch for more fruit to be born of the extension of Salesforce applications with AWS's raw resource powers. Hyperforce and Salesforce Functions are good indications of the future power that is constantly being added to the platform. AI is another area that Salesforce has quickly embraced, in the wake of the GPT hype storm; expect to see more of these rapid growth models increasing the options for your business.

Notably missing from the Salesforce offerings are data lake and data warehouse solutions. Since there isn't an ecosystem component branded and heralded here, you will want to provide oversight as to whether or not they are needed. Salesforce practitioners learn from the firehose of new functionality and renaming. If concepts don't make it into the firehose, they can get missed.

Another point to consider is stratification. Are you currently tied to a monolithic enterprise layout that is no longer a good fit? Are your resources overprovisioned and underutilized? You might benefit from the agility provided by smaller, loosely coupled systems, rather than maintaining a huge, unified infrastructure. Diversification is a powerful tool for business continuity, and fracturing your infrastructure to take more advantage of "swarm thinking" can add value.

Summary

Overall, the constraints of performance and resource management have kept Salesforce functionality in something of a gilded cage—but only in regard to being a true hosting or cloud replacement. There are definitely some considerations to be aware of with regard to *how* you implement data architectures in Salesforce. Almost all the critical components for any functionality are ready, almost ready, or being acquired. With all of the mentioned additions, the question is no longer *if* Salesforce could be your sole cloud resource vendor, but *when*. It's only a matter of time before an "Enable Quantum Processing" checkbox shows up in Setup somewhere. Also note that while the labels listed in Figure 4-1 are the examples that are usually the most talked about or marketed, there are plenty of worthy alternatives for each item, and many firms specialize in those alternatives. Savvy architects can make anything work at this point. The only crucial ingredients are having the budget and skillset to plan, implement, and manage Salesforce implementations. The bigger question is whether you are at a tipping point that is aligned with the maturity of Salesforce's offerings, and thus whether it's time to consider replatforming.

CHAPTER 5

Middleware and Connectivity

We've already discussed some of the systems involved in moving data into and out of the Salesforce ecosystem, but in this chapter we will look at the actual endpoints for connecting to that data. The most important thing to know about Salesforce connectivity is that you have to do almost everything with web service calls.

This chapter leans heavily on the concept of APIs. Broadly speaking, an API is any interface used to expose or share an application or system's data outside of itself in a programmatic fashion. There are many types of APIs: some require running on the same machine as the source system, some can be accessed over the web or HTTP. There are no accessible APIs that allow you to process Salesforce platform data without going through an HTTP-based API. Representational State Transfer (REST) is the preferred HTTP method, but some Simple Object Access Protocol (SOAP) interfaces persist. This can present some interesting challenges for enterprise architects that are accustomed to having a larger suite of patterns at their disposal natively. For example, automated processing of data in file format is not a feature of the core platform. There are many ways to achieve file processing with additional components or purchases, but not natively. (Data Loader, for example, is a free Java application maintained and distributed by Salesforce that can be installed on a server to parse files and push the data in them into Salesforce, using web service calls.) Salesforce's functional ecosystem is expanding at an exciting pace. Salesforce Functions and the platform event bus hint at the large-scale direction that will enable more enterprise-capable solutioning.

For Aspiring Architects

In the world of Salesforce practitioners, the word *architect* has a lot of different uses (we'll look at more of them in Chapter 11). One distinction that is sometimes made is between a *technical architect*, who may focus on initial setup and one-time configuration of elements that possibly work with external systems, and a *solution architect*, who focuses on planning and building internal functionality. Figure 5-1 illustrates some of the roles and duties of technical architects and solution architects (using a simplified definition of each). There's a lot of overlap between the two. The technical architect has other important functions, but integrations with other systems are one of the main differentiators. The technical architect will also tend to work on things once, establish a pattern or approach, and move on.

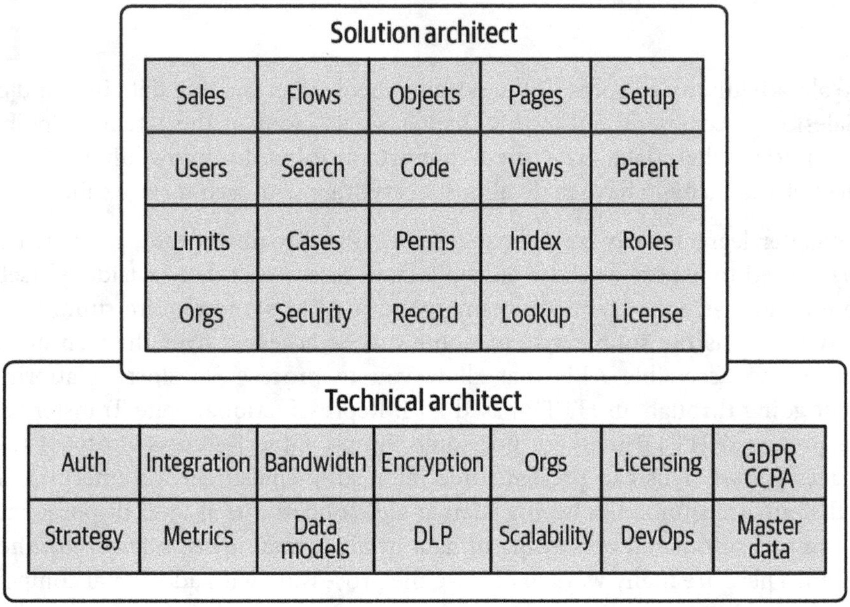

Solution architect

Sales	Flows	Objects	Pages	Setup
Users	Search	Code	Views	Parent
Limits	Cases	Perms	Index	Roles
Orgs	Security	Record	Lookup	License

Technical architect

Auth	Integration	Bandwidth	Encryption	Orgs	Licensing	GDPR CCPA
Strategy	Metrics	Data models	DLP	Scalability	DevOps	Master data

Figure 5-1. Role distribution for solution architects and technical architects

In Salesforce, there are more and more system integrations that can be done without having to deal with external system complexities. As an example, sending emails via Salesforce doesn't require any understanding or configuration of mail servers or relays. Email is effectively fully integrated into the Salesforce platform. Salesforce will continue to bring additional third-party functionality into the core platform, reducing the effort required to use it.

An *enterprise architect* tends to make comparisons across multiple systems (features, functionality, stability, cost) in order to build the optimal solution. As you expand your knowledge, pay attention to what each system does well. Also learn what your organization is efficient at implementing or managing. If you combine this with your knowledge of the costs involved in connecting to some other system, you will know when to create an integration. Customization, reliability, licensing, support, speed, complexity, and security are a few of the factors that should influence your decisions. For connecting to or from Salesforce, you will need to understand the different endpoints that connections will access coming in or out. Each endpoint may speak a different language or have other differentiating features that you should understand in order to know when to use them in or exclude them from your solutions.

Outbound: Server-Side Calls

Outbound connections from the Salesforce server only take a few fundamentally different pathways. The most common of these outbound data push or data fetch pathways are defined in Apex calls. Apex is the programming language primarily involved in any data manipulation customization within Salesforce (see Chapter 8). Apex calls create web service calls, either explicitly or by referencing configuration settings for outbound resources (the latter being the preferred method for security and maintenance).

Apex can process outbound requests synchronously or asynchronously. Asynchronous requests are sometimes referred to as "future methods" because of the way the callouts are labeled in code (@future). Internal and external data actions are governed (limited) to prevent overuse of shared I/O. Asynchronous requests are allowed more leeway than synchronous requests, so you should expect to spend extra effort if you need transactional integrity or sequential processing. One big caveat is that asynchronous calls are queued for execution across multiple tenants, and they can be highly variable in their execution times.

Owing to the increasing integrations with Marketing Cloud and other Salesforce-adjacent platforms like Snowflake, Slack, and Tableau, you may also consider outbound and inbound connections from those platforms as first-order endpoints. Marketing Cloud Customer Data Platform (CDP, recently rebranded as Genie) and Salesforce Functions have some very tight integrations with the Salesforce platform and can also effectively "share" data.

Salesforce Genie is effectively an enhanced graph-type service connected across different data partners and Salesforce instances. You can think of it as enabling data virtualization and relationship mapping across systems. It connects the data shared between the systems together to provide the most accurate version, regardless of where it was updated most recently. Tools for building systems based on graph architectures have been slow to reach maturity due to reliance on too many points of failure. Salesforce will likely have architected redundancy into this infrastructure, ensuring better results. The original functionality that was meant to bridge different systems—primarily those of the same customer from Marketing Cloud and any other

Salesforce system—was called *Customer 360*. The product was then renamed CDP and started to include other systems. Now known as Genie, with its rabbit mascot, it is being marketed as a holistic solution for any data, not just customer concepts. The performance for a system of virtual joins will be interesting to learn about, because latency is a challenge with this type of system. It can work fast, if you have a copy of the data somewhere to flatten or maintain join metadata like statistics and indexes. It can even be real-time, if you have highly responsive systems to provide data *and* have a fast system to do all the join operations. I'm not aware of an existing architecture that has built a successful foundation for this to reuse, however. If there is a healthy and scalable base system, this could be an industry-changing platform, especially if the claim of it being "zero-copy" is true.

Salesforce Functions will probably reach high levels of seamless integration in the near future. It's also very likely that certain Apex functions will leverage the new compute infrastructure, solely dependent on a predictive estimate of where the work would best be done. Salesforce Functions will effectively be a new headless compute entity that will be able to call outside data or call back into Salesforce data. Just like our email example, Salesforce Functions will likely be seamlessly integrated, but there may be some minor differences in the outbound endpoint or calls since it is technically originating from the headless stack.

 When establishing inbound integration patterns, it is best to maintain sessions as much as possible for multiple calls from your remote system. Not only can authentications slow down calls, but logins are counted as a separate governed resource unit in addition to connections.

Inbound: Remote System Calls

There are multiple ways to access Salesforce data from remote systems. The overwhelming majority of data and metadata within Salesforce is available or accessible via API calls (*https://oreil.ly/esteo*) that are all exposed by default. The most common pattern after that is to create accessible data endpoints with Apex code. Apex is able to initiate any actions within the Salesforce platform. The endpoint code called by remote systems can be run as *root* (unlimited administrator access), or you can enforce user permissions based on the credentials used by the calling service.

Endpoints can use the XML-based SOAP or the more flexible REST. There are automatically created endpoints that expose most of the information that you might need, and you can also create endpoints manually with custom code. It's very easy to label pieces of code to expose them as endpoints—almost too easy, as a lot of practice is required to secure those endpoints properly. The annotation used to designate code for external consumption is `@AuraEnabled`. You are able to expose different types of authentication protocols to different sets of users, which adds additional consumption options for your data.

Salesforce provides a very comprehensive library of integration patterns (*https:// oreil.ly/CO_X-*) for reference.

Client (Browser) Side

There are two main ways to reach out to data from the client side: iframes and Asynchronous JavaScript and XML (Ajax). Both of these pose potential security risks, and code that relies on them is subject to security changes by both IT departments and browser makers that can cause it to break. While users' browsers are able to make calls via Ajax and JavaScript, reducing latency and the server-borne request load, there are a lot of reasons to avoid this pattern. If your browser is surfing one domain and calling data from another, this is called *cross-site scripting* (XSS). XSS is a common hacking vector; to protect users from it, makers of browsers like Chrome and Safari have made the rules for pulling code or data from sites other than the one you intended to visit more and more restrictive.

Figure 5-2 illustrates the trade-off in load and complexity between server-side and client-side patterns. Note that with the client-side approach, you wouldn't want to pass any credentials to the browser so that it can authenticate to the external data source. You can exchange a token that can be used as a temporary credential, but this is extra work as well.

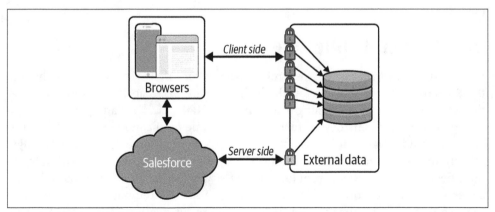

Figure 5-2. Client-side data calls versus server-side calls

On top of that, if the data call fails for any reason, you will have to include additional logic to process the failure. This makes the user's browser a network node in the application architecture, and you will have to secure and verify all possible points of access. VPNs and other such user networking complexities can also cause failures, and you'll need to deal with the challenge of getting the JavaScript call to be appropriately authenticated for the user's session. All of this will require a lot of custom coding. Only pursue this avenue if your use case warrants the effort and long-term maintenance costs.

Middleware

Since Salesforce is based on common standards, most third-party middleware systems will work well with Salesforce. There are several middleware system vendors that specialize in Salesforce and have polished, supported methods for moving data in and out with little work or experimentation required. Jitterbit, Boomi, and Informatica have all seen success in the Salesforce space as iPaaS providers.

Since its acquisition, MuleSoft has become one of the most talked about middleware components in the Salesforce ecosystem. MuleSoft provides a great deal of functionality: it's an API orchestration tool that is capable of performing a wide range of endpoint interactions as well as ETL functions. With sufficient development time you can write Apex code to execute most of these functions yourself, but it's much easier to keep track of complex integrations with specialty toolsets.

The entire concept of middleware is evolving, and few true "middleware-only" services exist today. Most of them have started to include other services, like message bus and data management capabilities. In addition, Salesforce has implemented quite a few direct connections to data management provider Snowflake, which could reduce the reliance on middleware to manage connections to data systems outside the core platform.

Event-Driven Architecture

Event-driven architecture (EDA) is a robust data pattern that is starting to take hold in the Salesforce ecosystem. Salesforce's platform event bus is an internal implementation of a very powerful streaming platform called Kafka. Kafka is an open source system that has a long history of fueling high-volume application designs. With this technology at its core, Salesforce instances are able to send large volumes of messages reliably to distributed systems. This message pathway and other enterprise integrations decouple your system from low- to mid-scale patterns and equip you to handle larger volumes of data in the future. It does take some forethought to decide when EDA should be implemented, but once you've created the foundation for an event architecture the development process should be relatively similar to the traditional work.

Figure 5-3 is an illustration of classic versus event-driven design patterns. Traditionally, you focus first on building a working system. Then, if the data it produces becomes so popular that the demand starts to negatively affect the system, you bolt on additional functionality to serve those requests. This may require rewriting a lot of core functionality. With an event-driven design approach user experience is still at the forefront, but immediately after considering the interface you think about other ways that the data may be useful. Is it relevant only in the context of that application, or is it something that will be valuable information for other systems? Early designation of data that is bound to be master data or an event that is or signals valuable data is key. Wiring to connect an event bus to an integration layer should already exist in most large enterprises. Third-party services also have data fabric offerings that can be canned solutions if you don't have a healthy high-volume middleware layer as a turnkey.

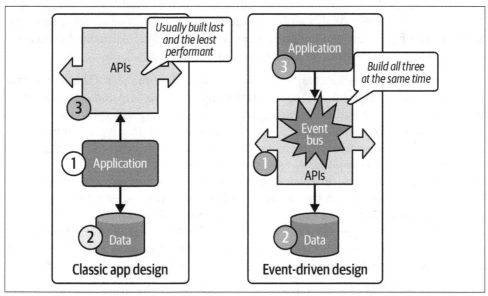

Figure 5-3. Classic versus event-driven application design

The other big consideration with events is transactional integrity. Many event-based systems are prone to message loss and order of operation unpredictability. This must be acceptable for your data model, or you need to build in protections. You almost always want to keep data flowing in as few unique pathways as possible, for simplicity and maintainability. However, using data keys and being able to utilize the bus to invoke transactional logic may be a necessity.

MuleSoft also has a message queue system that can participate in these larger distributed network patterns. Being able to move the functions of the event bus to different systems and focus different teams on different parts creates a lot of operational flexibility. In this scenario, different teams can use different tools and distribute the workload and responsibility.

OAuth

OAuth is a very common protocol used in Salesforce integrations. In the API key authorization model, the service endpoint provider creates a unique value and provides it to each individual consumer. For packages that connect to services outside of Salesforce this is often implemented as a *named credential*, in which the key is substituted for the password value and associated with a specific web URL. In this manner, each user of the service can only access it if their individual key is valid and the credential is scoped to a single URL endpoint, making it unusable for any other service. When implemented as part of a managed package deployment, there is no need to take the additional step of also setting up the endpoint URL. (For all other cases you must create one remote site endpoint in your org's settings.) All named credentials are automatically authorized for external communication.

The OAuth model is more complex to implement and administer. OAuth is a standardized framework that functions by establishing one or several *authorization granting authorities*. These authorities provide and validate a series of tokens and related permissions used by consumers to access defined resources. In a typical implementation, the org administrator will configure a credential that specifies the target external application URL. The application owner will provide a set of keys, one of which is a unique identifier and one of which is an encoded hash (commonly known as a client ID and client secret), which the org admin will store in the credential configuration. It is usually required that the consumer provide their public org URL to the application owner as part of a registration process to establish it as an authorized caller. The application can then call this URL for validation when a request is initiated (thus it is often known as a *callback* or *reply* URL).

Once a credential has been established and validated by the org administrator, any calls to the external application go through a back-and-forth token exchange process to establish the validity of the requestor's identity and permissions. The first time this occurs there is often a consent process in which the requester must accept a set of permission grants or scopes as defined by the external application, or, if calling back into the consumer's org, an available grant provided by Salesforce. These grants often must be renewed from time to time to ensure that only authorized access is being provided. Once the initial grant consent process has been completed, the two systems can begin the token exchange process, the result of which is a bearer or authorization token that can be used by the calling application to access the remote resource. This permits a flow of requests and responses without the need for continual authentication prompts; however, all such tokens have expiration periods and must be refreshed periodically, either administratively or through an interactive logon process.

Despite the increased complexity, OAuth is widely supported and is one of the most common methods in use for otherwise unrelated web applications to exchange data. It is important to note that the OAuth process does not capture, analyze, or validate any user passwords; it is not an authentication scheme but rather an authorization scheme, allowing already authenticated users to authorize communication between systems they have access to, and only when such access as has been defined in the explicit permission grants. While not foolproof, it is more secure than a simple exchange of key/value pairs, and it's much less prone to exploitation than other legacy authorization mechanisms. It is not necessary to fully understand the inner workings of the OAuth token exchange process in order to implement it, and you may not need to use it any time soon. Still, knowing the basics of how it functions can make it easier to deploy, secure, and manage third-party solutions within your org or provide access to your data from other applications outside of Salesforce.

The Good

Middleware and connectivity is another very exciting part of the Salesforce ecosystem. Extremely powerful pieces of enterprise functionality are being released at a regular cadence. A recurring focus of this book is highlighting the new components of the ecosystem that move Salesforce from a sales automation platform to a fully fledged enterprise application and data platform. With each such development, the platform's ability to serve the full range of our organizational needs grows. Vertical integration can make enterprise architecture (EA) problems much easier to solve. These functions aren't Salesforce's bread-and-butter applications, but despite the relative lack of marketing and fanfare, many exist.

Communication about EA–level features is still nascent in the ecosystem, but it's improving; the Salesforce Architects website (*https://architect.salesforce.com*) and blog (*https://oreil.ly/Rcxzr*) are the best sources of this type of knowledge.

The Gotchas

High-volume data patterns have many additional complications that have to be accounted for. In Salesforce's consumption-based model, licensing can be expensive and difficult to forecast and track. Salesforce has a collaborative "true-up" model that can make charges less disruptive to the project goals. Regardless, understanding how your event signals are emitted and consumed can be difficult. For this reason, many people opt for a simpler unlimited model, trading more effort and possibly higher cost for predictability. Working in an environment where there are no consequences for unplanned growth can be a huge benefit as you are attempting to understand your scaling needs.

Since most event bus components are designed around speed and scale, security can be overlooked. DLP and intrusion detection (ID) systems may not be able to keep up with the data rates that event architectures support. Segmenting sensitive and less-sensitive data distinctly within your event architectures is highly recommended; the added security this allows you to provide for sensitive data is usually well worth the additional management effort.

Another problem with some EDA applications is validation. Unlike with a bulk nightly synchronization pattern, missed or failed event updates don't have an easy fix with the next night's full upload. This problem exists for incremental synchronization patterns too, but it can lead to distrust of your data. There are many checksum and error handling patterns that can mitigate this concern with a little more effort. Any time that data has enough value that missing any fraction of transactions causes angst, you can always switch to a transaction pattern or add error logic.

As with any system, there's no perfect calculator for determining how many of each type of possible transaction Salesforce can handle over a given time period. There are very detailed documents out there to guide you as you consider when you might be approaching a boundary and need to consider putting one of these force-multiplier patterns into use.

The Growth

As evidenced by the acquisitions of MuleSoft and Tableau, Salesforce sees a future in bigger data. Watch for Genie and big objects to also play a big role in moving solutions from narrowly targeted functions to enterprise-scale suites of functionality. Tableau and Snowflake are already in a class of their own, and the future will likely see more and more leveraging of the raw power of the AWS infrastructure.

Blockchain is one of the few areas that hasn't seen a major offering within the Salesforce ecosystem, but they may only be waiting to hear about more customer demand. This is another trustable interchange technology that has yet to have a big impact beyond digital currency but is likely to continue to work its way into business technology use cases.

Summary

In general practice, Salesforce is a good single pane of glass to surface data from remote systems easily. There are decades of history of systems being able to talk to Salesforce and have Salesforce pull remote data. With the application logic layer in between all inbound requests, it's definitely better to think in terms of events and atomic updates instead of using nightly sync patterns. There are bulk access and upload pathways (see Chapter 3), but those can get clunky.

There is definitely some art and many skills involved in getting systems talking to each other. With Salesforce, as long as you appropriately size your requests and operate within your limits or budget, this is all handled for you. Leveraging external powerhouse providers like AWS and Kafka is only really required when you are building extremely large systems. If you are already using those systems in your corporate ecosystem, you may need them for Salesforce. Salesforce scales well as needed and requires only some additional discipline to stay within some of its more stringent limits. For extremely large use cases there are other options, like dedicated instances, available. The biggest point to take home here is that connectivity, and in particular the connectivity that allows for massive scalability, is available and quite healthy in the Salesforce ecosystem. Salesforce is not just a simple application or application framework you will have to shoehorn functionality into; it's an entire highly scalable cloud ecosystem that happens to live under the banner of what was a simple application some 20 years ago. It has grown to the point where it has a competitive offering on par with every modern cloud provider in every critical IT area.

CHAPTER 6

Collaboration

The entirety of the Salesforce platform could be considered a collaboration suite (for the purposes of this chapter, we'll define collaboration as "end user to end user," where an end user can be a customer). But Salesforce is not a generic sharing tool; it's a rather specific sharing tool. The Sales Cloud functionality is at its core a way for salespeople to collaborate remotely with a central office. Salesforce added the Experience Cloud (formerly Community Cloud, a.k.a. "Communities") functions to enable even more granular collaboration between sales teams and customers. Salesforce objects like Contacts, Cases, Accounts, and Orders are all about sharing data with different sets of users.

Collaboration and social sharing have been very hot topics in the industry in the past decade. Digital transformations to empower self-service tools and collaboration have been widely debated, since it is extremely difficult to measure their value. The value proposition that each cloud offers involves its strengths and the other peripheral functions that it does well enough to keep you from having to buy other products. If you *need* Salesforce but not necessarily best-in-breed collaboration, you can probably save money and resources by staying inside this single vendor's offerings. Managing multicloud and multiple best-in-breed systems adds a management and resource penalty that is not insignificant. This is another tipping point that can help you determine when it is appropriate to move one way or the other.

Collaboration Is More Than Just Sharing

Within Salesforce there are several functional components that have broad sharing functions. These tools can be leveraged in a variety of ways. It's important to know that these less-discussed functions exist before you consider integrating one of the more popular versions that exist outside of the Salesforce ecosystem. They're a good fit for many designs, and knowing about them can help you decide when to use them and when to consider others. Figure 6-1 shows some conceptual groupings of the collaboration features in Salesforce to illustrate where they are relevant.

 Sharing in Salesforce tends to mean having permission to see data/ records. In the collaboration space, sharing is a bit more unbridled than Salesforce's record-by-record approach: it generally means being able to communicate about, cooperate on, and exchange multiple types of information.

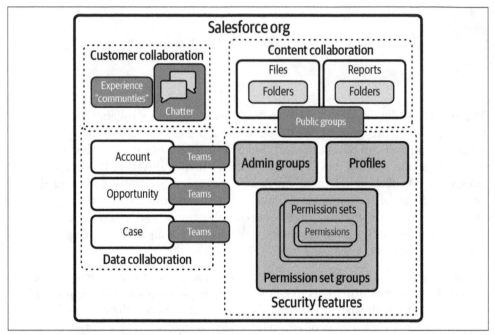

Figure 6-1. Salesforce core platform collaboration features

This figure also includes some permissions concepts that have similar names, for awareness. These concepts will be covered in depth in the next chapter.

Chatter

Chatter is the original collaboration and chat tool built into Salesforce. It enables sharing of files and information and group discussions, as well as tagging or follow-ing items and adding notes with a chat dialog style. Chatter is less of a standalone chat application than a messaging framework that is available within other functions. It's probably most easily likened to Yammer or Disqus. Most of the time, Chatter is used to add notes and comments to specific records or items in Salesforce. There is also an option to put comments into a central forum within applications, or org-wide.

Chatter was hard to get excited about because the web-based controls are just not as dense as those provided by other chat systems, like Slack (now also part of Salesforce, and discussed later in this chapter), Messenger, or Teams. Also, the fact that Chatter is embedded into the Salesforce interface, so it's never used on its own, may have contributed to people preferring other, more focused chat tools.

Groups

There are two implementations of user "groups" within Salesforce. Both refer to lists of users: one is a private, administrator-controlled selection of users, and the other is a public, user-created list of collaborators. The public group function relates to sharing files, reports, and records within the application. There are programmatic ways to synchronize both types of groups with external control systems, but these user groups have a fairly specific coupling to Salesforce record functions. Because of this, equating Salesforce groups with standard access control lists (ACLs) is seldom appropriate.

Permission set groups (PSGs) in Salesforce are highly reusable and can easily be mapped to other enterprise systems of record. PSGs are groups of permissions based on a job function, to which members can be added. Those members could be considered a group, but that's not how they are labeled or referred to within Salesforce circles. Think of groups as a small component of permission functionality and a separate small component of data sharing among users. Salesforce has a great deal of granularity in permissions, and the number of terms to learn can be overwhelming!

Teams

Not to be confused with the chat and collaboration tool Microsoft Teams, *teams* in Salesforce are very similar to the groups described in the previous section. Salesforce implementations are commonly focused on three goals: Account management, Opportunity management, and Case management. These are all core functions of sales and service, as well as being key objects within the Salesforce data model. If more than one person is working on any given record or associated records of these objects, you have the option of creating a team of users, who may have different rights. "Account teams," "Opportunity teams," and "Case teams" are common collaboration and sharing functions in those sales and service work processes. Teams are usually administered by users in a certain role and not a system administrator.

 Cases or *tickets* are part of the core Salesforce platform, which provides a decent set of useful functionality. Service Cloud provides a large set of enhanced capabilities on top of the base Case functionality. Service Cloud is a licensed package add-on for your Salesforce org. It revolves around Cases, but you can use Cases without having Service Cloud.

Files

Files (formerly referred to as attachments) and *Salesforce Files* are another set of terms that could be confusing to some. All object records can be configured to have files (documents) associated with them. There were originally two different backend binary object storage methods, but these have since been merged in the backend. When files are uploaded, they can be associated with multiple records or have their access granted to multiple users. Associating a file with a record does not make a copy of it; the file content is independent of the associations.

The term *Salesforce Files* refers to the newer backend technology for file storage, which adds the concept of folders for organization and sharing. Folders can be shared in the same way that files can. Since sharing relationships and folder structures are data elements and not related to a filesystem, it's very easy to work with them and rearrange them. The actual file content itself is not as easy to code around.

Salesforce Files work fine for most use cases, but you can run into hurdles when trying to program with them. File data is currently stored in database item storage, and that leads to some size and throughput constraints. The ability to manipulate database data in memory is also limited on the platform, and this can cause challenges in circumstances like copying, appending, reading, and testing. Salesforce encourages more complex or large file storage requirements to be met on platforms like Amazon S3. There are many connectors that enable this almost seamlessly, without much effort.

Reports

Similar to files, reports and dashboards can be created inside the platform and shared via *report folders*. Though they work the same way, these are a different type of logical container than the folders used for files. That means you won't ever see a folder with both reports and files in it. Reports aren't used much for collaboration, at least not in an interactive sense, but due to the similar folder construct that is used to manage them, it seemed appropriate to reference them here.

Quip

Quip is an acquisition that has been getting very slowly integrated into the platform over the last few years. Quip itself is an entire collaboration platform that has similar functionality to Google Docs or Microsoft Office Online. Documents can be shared and used as wiki pages, and there's a local desktop or mobile application that supports working offline. There's also a chat and messaging function built into Quip that is separate from Chatter. Quip isn't intended to be used as a bulk file storage system, for the same reason as Salesforce Files. However, this can be viewed as a solid new "mobile office" component as the world returns to a commuting habit and re-embraces mobile productivity. For a simplified comparison, Figure 6-2 shows a functional representation of the standout features of Quip.

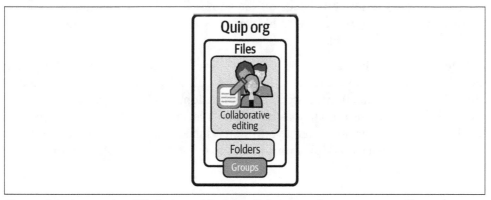

Figure 6-2. A very simplified view of Quip's collaboration features

Slack

Slack is a widely used team and group chat and collaboration system, recently acquired by Salesforce. As it rose to popularity with developers, it caused a mindset shift that no one was expecting: "chat-centric productivity." Slack reverses the concept of chat in apps, and instead brings apps to chat. This reversal may not sit as well with the lifestyle of highly conversant and collaborative people as it does with those that are heads-down most of the day and want to be able to filter out distractions. Slack has support for audio and video calling built in, as well as for variants like "huddles," which are ongoing calls that you can join/leave any time (Figure 6-3).

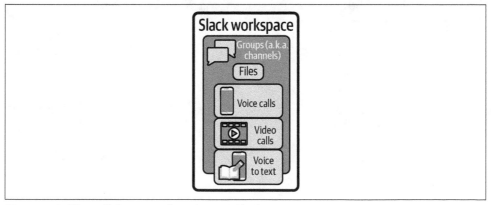

Figure 6-3. The collaboration functions in Slack

Another key feature of Slack is the way that it integrates other applications. Application notifications can either come in as independent message channels or inline with your current chat windows. Calendar or meeting reminders don't pop up in other windows, requiring you to break focus and multitask. Another focus-harnessing function is that Slack leans in to typing keywords to perform other functions. This reduces the need to lift your hands off the keyboard and start mousing. It's kind of like when you finally install an ad blocker on your browser; the serenity of noise reduction is quickly tangible.

Salesforce has promised that it will embrace a Slack-first reimagining of all its products. I interpret this to mean data prompts and calls to action will take a back seat to the primary work function of users. This migration to a curated experience rather than multiple panes of pulsating alerts will do a lot for the industry of information workers. I love hearing about new hybrid systems that combine search and data into a single-line call. I hope other platforms lean in to this cleaning up of worker interfaces as well.

The Good

Salesforce has a lot of functionality enabling you to share specific information with specific people or groups. Figure 6-4 gives an overview of what's inside the circle and reusable, and what strengths you might need to seek elsewhere.

Quip is a product that has some functional parity with SharePoint or OneDrive, in addition to its web-based document editing functions. Slack seems to be set to compete with Teams for communication, but I'm not sure if it will tackle the file sharing capabilities of Teams/SharePoint in the near term. Experience Cloud (Community) does seem to be regularly adding more collaboration functions, enabling customer-to-representative and even customer-to-customer communication as well as providing interactive knowledge and resources that can reduce support efforts and increase satisfaction. This will be an interesting space to watch.

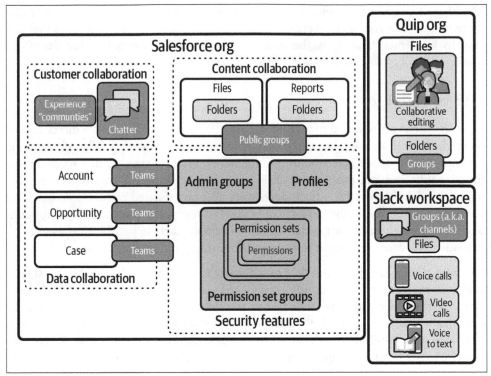

Figure 6-4. Distribution of collaboration functionality in the core Salesforce platform

The Gotchas

Salesforce's ecosystem is about sharing information, but in very intentional and structured ways. The company's investments and roadmap all seem to focus on this, with the exception of the Slack acquisition. Expect the focus on Slack's "quality of life" slant to work its way through the platform in subtle ways. Efforts to enable water-cooler interactions and self-governed libraries will probably continue to thrive only in tools like SharePoint, Confluence, and Facebook. Considering the number of ways there already are to share data within Salesforce, it's probably a good thing to not have an unmanaged area to police as well.

With collaboration comes greater risk of accidental oversharing. Salesforce has only enabled collaboration features whose value greatly outweighs their risk, but regular reviews of the achieved value of those risky capabilities should be conducted. Making sure you keep up with how much freedom you are giving users to influence data exposure is key. Be modern and flexible, but be sure to review, track, and communicate your risks.

The biggest challenge in trying to look at Salesforce in terms of collaboration is that there is no single cohesive governing model. You can share in so many ways that it is easy to lose track. Hopefully the promise of a Slack-first reboot of the Salesforce workspace will make collaboration a more cohesive story.

The Growth

With the focus on resource management, organic operations without a direct impact on the bottom line (like sales) will probably remain a low priority for Salesforce going forward. Expect to see investments in integrations to other systems that focus on this functionality and can enable it at scale without sacrificing the multitenant performance model. Support for citizen developers and unregulated intranets and sharing seems to have cooled in the industry over the past few years, due to the need for content and oversight in almost equal measure. Content starts to get "bad" as soon as it's uploaded and must be curated to keep from becoming out-of-date noise.

AI could change the game and do a much better job of finding the newest, most relevant content from among multiple unregulated sources. Look for investments in conversational AI to change the landscape of anything that used to depend on search or organization and/or findability patterns. If AI is allowed to pull information from chat logs and publications, the need to compile information into documents may soon be in the rearview. Adjust your roadmaps accordingly.

Summary

It is very important to note that I'm only covering here the native features of the core platform and the more collaboration-focused products, like Quip and Slack. Some third-party add-ons are used so often they are almost native. Many of these features have their own license costs associated with them, so while they may be native, they are not always free. It's always a good idea to confirm that the features you think you are getting are included in your purchases and also have the usage capacity you are expecting.

The purpose of outlining all of these sharing and collaboration features is to expose how many boxes are checked in Salesforce, compared to dedicated collaboration platforms. If you want generic and semistructured file sharing or documentation, you can look outside of Salesforce's core offerings. If you want a thoughtful and surgical application of sharing and communication, you can get that done with the features described here. Licensing for the larger components, like file storage and Slack, will continue to evolve. This should allow you to select your collaboration functions à la carte instead of wading into the massive landscapes of Confluence or SharePoint. Those systems and others like them are fantastic for intelligence-based organizations but require a lot of work to govern and secure. Precise functionality can be much more cost-efficient and manageable.

CHAPTER 7

Security

Working in a very complex cloud environment with a very flexible platform requires a lot of focus on security design and maintenance. Much of Salesforce's success is based on how easy it is to share information with teammates and coworkers. The myriad ways you can configure permissions provide lots of utility for users and developers. However, there are at least three different areas you should continuously monitor to guard against oversharing and unnecessary exposure. We're going to cover three security paradigms here, with the important observation that these three patterns interact and that "effective" permissions are the sum of the permissions the same user or role has on each system. We'll also be discussing the internal mechanisms for handling permissions in Salesforce, and some common misconceptions that arise from not fully appreciating some of the ways permissions work.

 Salesforce security concept #1: Just because you cannot see a piece of data does not mean you cannot access it. There are native web services and pages that exist by default that can show you any data that you have been granted access to. It is a common security hole that objects and data are created and manipulated by automation in a way that is not intended to be seen by the user. A common misstep is to overshare data when trying to enable anonymous (unauthenticated) access on Experience Cloud sites (Communities). Flows and other visual tools that require read access to a record by a hidden query are accessing public data. Just because you don't display a record doesn't ensure that a permission is not exposing all records to all visitors.

Single Sign-on

Salesforce supports single sign-on (SSO), which allows users to authenticate securely with multiple applications using one set of credentials, and it can be accessed using any modern federated identity system (Azure Active Directory, Okta, Ping, etc.). Salesforce can also act as a federated identity provider for other systems. This means that you can use your company's current computer or identity system to log in to Salesforce, with no additional password to remember. For security mavens, it also means that you can deactivate identities in your central system and they will be unable to log in to Salesforce thereafter. The federation setup for the Salesforce platform is very polished. Any engineer that knows their way around a certificate can configure an identity provider in a few minutes. The configuration screens also have a handy OAuth debug feature that makes troubleshooting minor issues simple.

> The acronym SSO has a few flavors. There's *single sign-on*, and then there's *same sign-on*. The terms are often conflated. The difference is that with single sign-on, once you authenticate and have an active session, you don't have to authenticate again. The session is detected from your browser or device and there's no password challenge. With same sign-on, you get a password challenge on different systems and have to give your username and password multiple times, but it's the same password (plus two-factor authentication, if required) each time.

Figure 7-1 gives an introduction to federated identity, which enables SSO to applications across domains or organizations. First, the Salesforce website/application communicates behind the scenes with another identity provider to share the responsibility of authentication. When you go to your Salesforce URL, you are redirected to your identity provider's website. You provide your credentials, and a session token cookie is added to your browser or device session. When you are directed back to Salesforce, Salesforce calls back to the identity provider and validates your token. Your token also carries an "assertion" of your identity from the provider that Salesforce uses to match you to a corresponding Salesforce user account (if one exists). The assertion and cookie are encrypted with tokens provided in the setup process. Encryption uses certificates, and certificates require regular renewal. It is very important to make sure your security team assumes oversight of this area.

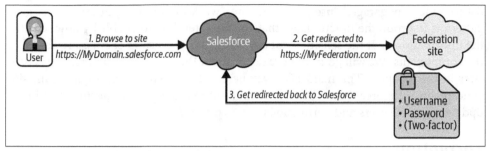

Figure 7-1. Basic federated identity process

Each sandbox where you want to use SSO will require its own certificate(s) as part of the federation setup. These certificates are included in the XML files used to do most setups, so you are never really handling a certificate on its own; it's part of the bundle. But if the certificates expire, the error messages can be less than obvious to administrators and users. It's best to have a reminder set to renew them before they cause problems.

Identity Management

Identity management (IDM) is a holistic practice centered around managing authentication and authorization across multiple applications. Federated identity is just one piece of the process. Managing authorization (what an authenticated user can do, access, or see) is an entirely different challenge. Security Authentication Markup Language 2.0 (SAML 2.0) is currently the most widely accepted standard for cross-domain authentication. There's still not a widely accepted standard for permissions and authorization, but the top-tier IDM providers are fluent with the container structures for permissions within Salesforce.

Breaking it down, within Salesforce you can create different structures of users and add users to them. You can also build structures of different types of "permissibles" (I'm not sure this is used as a noun outside the vernacular of my security architect friends!). A permissible is a unit of a permission that makes up an ability to do something. For example, the permission to "fix my car" might require the permissables of "enter my garage," "turn on my garage light," "open my car's hood," "work on my engine," "work on my alternator," "work on my spark plugs," and "use my tools." Each of these unique abilities might be configured in different places, but alone they don't make much sense. Also, you wouldn't want to fill out a form with or manage individual permission quanta; you'd want to address them at the level where a user would have some context about their function. While you're making it easy for the user to understand, don't forget to include some consideration of granularity. An appropriate appreciation of security boundary interactions would dictate simplifying the previous list to "enter my garage," "use my tools," and "work on anything in my car." A good pattern is to group the functionality that you are intending to enable by how sensitive the information is. If the sensitivity of any element in the group changes, review all of the components. We will go into more detail about the internal component structures later in this chapter. The main takeaway here is that there are multiple permission concepts in Salesforce. Your IDM tools will need to manage a connection and insert, update, or delete users and permissions.

Encryption

I see a fair amount of confusion around encryption on cloud platforms, and Salesforce is no exception. In Salesforce, all internet-facing endpoints use at least HTTPS encryption. Certificates and cryptography protect all channels into your Salesforce data. When integrating with Salesforce, you should make sure that every link in your data chain is encrypted. That is to say, you should secure every exposed piece of communication.

In addition to all of the inbound and outbound channels being covered, Salesforce offers column-level encryption for specific fields. Additional levels of security and file encryption should only be added to mitigate physical attacks on the hardware. For example, transparent data encryption (TDE) ensures that authorized users and applications can access the data as needed, but that if the servers or the files containing the data are stolen it won't be easily readable. Adding column-level encryption is similar to TDE in that the data is encrypted at the filesystem level but is decrypted whenever an authorized request is received.

Figure 7-2 illustrates the types of data that can be exposed and the locations that are most often the source of those exposures. You can see that some of the exposures involve a breach of physical locations that are not reasonably vulnerable in most cases. There are definitely some cases where every type of precaution is warranted, but make sure you understand all the potential risks and penalties as well as the benefits of securing each layer before you add them to your designs.

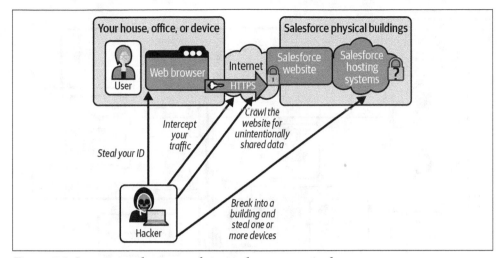

Figure 7-2. Locations where your data can be compromised

 As discussed in Chapter 4, Salesforce IDs may look like random GUIDs, but they are not. They are a combination of well-known codes that refer to objects (which are the same across every Salesforce customer) and some Base64-encoded autonumber values. Base64 encoding is reversible, and having access to a single URL can potentially give someone enough information to easily and almost invisibly read all of the records in a table. "Invisible" here means that a much less suspicious load is generated, since valid URLs can be guessed without guessing many wrong URLs. So don't see that URL string that looks random and assume that's any sort of hardening. It's the opposite.

Permission Containers

Figure 7-3 illustrates the different permission container concepts in Salesforce. For simplicity, I'm grouping these concepts to represent any situation where there is a clear set of users paired with some sort of access. In other contexts they are called access control lists. Some of the containers are direct person-to-resource structures, others are hierarchical, and some are extended further as container-to-container-to-container structures.

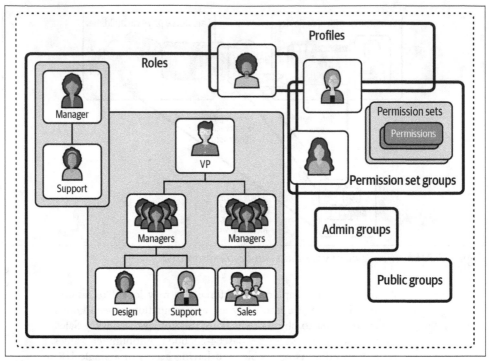

Figure 7-3. Examples of permission container concepts on the platform

We go into more detail in the following subsections, but it is important to understand that they all play off of each other.

Profiles

Profiles are the original permission containers for Salesforce. Profiles came into being when the platform was really just a sales application. Salesforce has grown the concept to try and fit modern models, but they're a little rigid owing to their simple start. Profiles enable five primary pieces of user access control: license use, feature use, object (table) access, login class, and system admin access. They're the first tier of access control within Salesforce, and they're a bit of a blunt tool. The biggest drawback of the profile is that users can only be assigned to a single profile. Profiles show their age when trying to provision users with varying access levels across different application functionality built into the platform.

Each profile has to be assigned to a *license* available on your instance per your Salesforce contract agreement. For instance, you might have purchased 100 platform (basic) user licenses and 20 enhanced licenses (e.g., Service Cloud licenses). Each user you create will need to be assigned to a profile, and each profile is assigned to a license type. Once you've assigned profiles to all of your available licenses, you cannot assign any more, so managing and reassigning licenses to active users can be a regular exercise.

Features purchased in addition to the standard platform license, like Service Cloud or Knowledge, are also enabled via profile settings. The more features you purchase or that are included in the platform for free, the more checkboxes there are to manage inside each profile.

Object access control is another major role of the profile. Each object is listed for enablement in the profile settings at the Create, Read, Edit, Delete (CRED, a.k.a. CRUD) level only. Remember, an object is an entire table, not just a single record. As you build more applications in Salesforce, one of the key patterns is reusing objects to hold more than just one type of data. You might want a user to have read access to Accounts of type X, have read/write access to Accounts of type Y, and have no access to Accounts of type Z; this cannot be fully implemented exclusively with profiles. There are more granular permission structures within Salesforce that can also enable object access, but while you can use these other structures to provide narrower access to data, you can't use them to narrow access to an object to which a user has already been granted profile-level access. This means that any well-planned permission structure can be undone by an errant grant.

Profiles control certain security concepts as well that I'll refer to collectively as the *login class*. The powerful system administrator role is granted inside of the profile. You need to manage your count of system administrators with your overall Salesforce licensing. For other types of users, profiles let you control access nuances like IP range and login hour restrictions. Users with these restrictions can authenticate but be denied access if they are coming from an unapproved network or geographic location. Login hours additionally restrict logins to certain times of the day or weekend when approved users are permitted to access the system.

While profiles served with distinction in the past, complex application platform usage has outgrown them. Profiles are a necessary licensing and administrative control feature, but the fine-grained permission controls they provide are clunky. Hopefully profiles will continue to shed fine-grained functions in deference to permission set groups (which we'll discuss shortly). Ongoing practice should be to make the profiles as generic as possible, separating users by license type and login class, then use other structures to control data access and permissioning.

Roles

Roles is another term that has a few connotations within the Salesforce platform, one of which is specific to permissions and security structures. Roles do not map to the R in RBAC (role-based access control). Rather, roles in the context of Salesforce security and permissions are used to define small-scale, low-depth user *hierarchies* that share certain data or records. Examples would be *manager*, *direct report*, and *peer*. That mini-tree has three branches that are what Salesforce calls roles. Your position in a role hierarchy is your role.

Behind the scenes, roles are a complex waterfall structure viewed through a simple UI. Role hierarchies should be used sparingly, and only where ensuring inheritance or record access "survival" is vital. There's no need to mirror the company's entire org chart in role hierarchies; they should host only the parts of the structure that are absolutely key to managing data that is in Salesforce. Roles shouldn't be used to acknowledge status changes or promotions, but only to indicate the level of data access that a user or group of users requires. They should only be reassigned when a change in access is absolutely necessary. Individuals at different levels in the org chart can and often do share the same role. In fact, you might only need two roles that appear at the *same* tier: say, one for VPs to share purchase approvals and a second top-tier branch for phone agents to share case notes. If there's no reason to nest those groups within each other, don't do it. This minimizes the backend waterfall effects caused by changes to either group.

Figure 7-4 is a simple example to help you visualize how quickly a role change can amplify, causing many sharing records to be created and deleted. At a large scale, sharing recalculation can harm performance, slowing down your instance.

Everything shared with Luis is shared with Paul.
Everything shared with Paul is shared with Lara.

Granted by	User	Object	Access
Profile	Luis	Account object	Read/write
Manual share	Luis	Single contact record	Read/write
Manual share	Luis	Another contact record	Read/write
Team role (works with Luis)	Paul	Account object	Read/write
HR role (manages Paul)	Lara	Account object	Read/write
Role (works with Luis)	Paul	Single contact record	Read/write
Role (reports to Paul)	Lara	Single contact record	Read/write
Rule (works with Luis)	Paul	Another contact record	Read/write
Role (reports to Paul)	Lara	Another contact record	Read/write

If Luis changed teams, all of these permission records would be deleted and MANY new ones would be created for all his new teammates and their managers.

Figure 7-4. Roles lead to sharing records having a snowball effect

Permissions, Permission Sets, and Permission Set Groups

The *permissions* structure in Salesforce is the one that you will want to focus most on. It aligns to more traditional application permission strategies, which means better interoperability with mature identity and access management (IAM) systems. Being able to easily map a Salesforce permission to an external approval and review process is key. If you were using profiles, your permission "handles" would be paired to licensing and not actual system permissions.

Permission sets are collections of permissions and settings that determine access to tools, functions, services, and resources provided by the Salesforce platform. Permission set groups are a fairly recent security model that enables different permission sets to be grouped together so that they can be easily assigned to certain users. Not all IAM systems support permission set groups, but as their use increases, the integrations will follow.

From an EA perspective, you don't need to know much detail about these concepts except that they are different from and more extensible than profiles and roles. Salesforce makes it easy to roll out that first application, but some extra time is needed to build a good security- and compliance-friendly permission model that can grow with you. Look to your other employee systems to find which existing models or persona/role definitions should be mirrored by your Salesforce implementation. It should be *very* rare to onboard an application/function that serves a completely new group of users. Building a shared model decreases training time and data leak potential.

Manual Sharing

The previous sections described the primary strategies for creating and maintaining security containers in the UI. There are also record-by-record means to grant access. Users with certain permissions can decide to share them with other users in the system. These permissions don't survive if that user loses access to those records, though, and the permission to grant permissions to others can be controlled if desired. Developers can also grant access directly to individual records without adhering to the visible structures created in the UI.

Behind the scenes, there are two ways to determine who has permission to see a record: precalculated and just-in-time (JIT). With *precalculated* permissions, there is a sharing record directly attached to the record you want to see that says you are allowed to see it. For precalculation to work, the permissions of all users needs to be recalculated when any change that affects user access is made. That change triggers the deletion and re-creation of the sharing records attached to the affected object records. With JIT permissions, when you try to access an object, another system (or multiple systems) is consulted to see if you should be given access. Essentially, they're both doing the same thing, except for the additional latency and layers required to determine whether to approve your access query with JIT permissions (versus the instant answer you get with precalculated permissions).

 While it can be necessary and/or quicker to use programmatic or ad hoc sharing, you *must* invest the time to properly document your off-the-map data sharing structures. It's not easy to review and troubleshoot security model problems, even with expensive scanning tools. Salesforce administrators and programmers are also very seldom in charge of holistic data security patterns, so do your best to make it easy for those who are.

Effective Permissions

All of the preceding information set the stage for the concept of *effective permissions*. Since each permission is additive, effective permissions are the matrix product of all of the previously discussed permission-granting systems added together. Since profiles, roles, groups, teams, and permission set groups are not exclusive, combinatorics come into play. The flexibility of different permission structures leads to complexity when they overlap (Figure 7-3 shows some of the ways that this can happen). If you are trying to manage permissions with an RBAC or IAM system, the permutations of groups multiplied by groups can lead to potential oversharing.

From the user up, the premise is simple: the user's access is the sum of the access of all the groups they are a member of. Trying to manage it by role/group means that every area of overlap is effectively another role/group to manage. There is a new breed of tools that can help you analyze this space, but bear in mind that it's best to have a very good holistic security model in place before you take on any major project with any sort of sensitive data.

The Good

The Salesforce core platform allows for extremely granular control of what data is shared and with whom. Builders and administrators have access to a variety of sharing and restriction patterns to use to properly share information and work. Most of the containers for users are easy to understand and expose to an IDM system. The platform is also very easy to integrate into all major federated identity systems for SSO. Most of the other aspects that need to be surveyed regularly are easily exposed to tools specific to the task.

The security framework started strong in Salesforce, and the ecosystem seems to be growing to match the threat landscape. We should see more tools like Shield's Einstein Data Detect (EDD) grow to use AI to intelligently monitor data for potential problems. EDD is specific to Salesforce, but this flavor of DLP is not. We need more systems capable of doing this across different platform stacks as part of a holistic strategy. Some of the titans in the DLP, SaaS security posture management (SSPM), and cloud access security broker (CASB) space are starting to include Salesforce monitoring in their offerings.

The Gotchas

The overwhelming flexibility of Salesforce is the only thing to worry about. "Effective permissions" review and management will be a big part of conscientious IT professionals' work, across many job functions. Salesforce brings more than the usual share of complexity to manage for a single application—even more than for the average application platform. Plus, it is growing. Here we are only talking about the core platform. The other acquisitions and platforms also have their own security paradigms that don't necessarily align to the core permission structures described here. Security-focused architects will need to carefully plan the approved methods of granting access. Keeping those plans visible and manageable by security and compliance teams will require good investment in architects and communication.

Iterative design is another pattern that can cause trouble in heavily customized organizations. The first planned iteration should spend time documenting the entire near- and long-term pattern for permissions and security. Unfortunately, the available tools for visualizing and managing all the different ways to provide access to functions and information within the platform are currently immature. There are literally dozens of places to check to understand where information can go. Gaining awareness of the entire permission-scape can challenge even the most apt Salesforce architects. Sharing these concepts with InfoSec professionals can be even more challenging. Cooperation and understanding the unfamiliar and overlapping security structures is key to maintaining a secure platform.

The Growth

There's another product/service you can add to your environment, called Salesforce Shield (thankfully, it isn't called the Security Cloud… yet). The security and compliance features of this product are growing every year. There are also many third-party scanning and mitigation tools that are maturing rapidly in the same space. Leveraging all of these tools is becoming table stakes for any large company or companies that value their data security. Look for this space to continue to rapidly evolve along with Salesforce and its close integrations and acquisitions. Application builders and developers are not necessarily skilled at both the fastest way to get something done and the most secure way to get something done. Fortunately, toolsets that can help mitigate this are maturing and becoming more widely available.

Summary

The popularity and ubiquity of Salesforce have made it a favored target for hackers. There are many popular scripts designed to easily start scanning a Salesforce org for exposed information. Customization and even basic administration of Salesforce can lead to accidentally oversharing information that hackers can find. This might not be a worry for small organizations without confidential information at their core. Salesforce applications can be quickly built and secured provided they use only a few permission concepts. Once you move beyond those first simple applications, however, you should carefully plan your security strategy and create checkpoints to confirm that strategy stays intact.

CHAPTER 8

Programming and Customization

This chapter covers programming and customization of Salesforce. Many readers will be familiar with the concepts discussed here, because these tools are already present in their organization/operations. These readers may be seeking more knowledge about how they combine and how they are different.

It should not be assumed that you will have to use code to customize the platform. You might eventually, but in order to quickly take advantage of all the new features and feature upgrades, you should strive to use as many of them "out of the box" as possible. You shouldn't start customizing unless you're sure there isn't an existing pre-built feature that you can leverage (including newly released features). Your solution engineers should be able to meet the vast majority of your incoming needs without code. The flexible and modern programming features that have been added to the platform can be almost too enticing, but you'll reap long-term benefits by reducing your customizations and leaning into the art of the possible within the existing platform functions, without extending into code.

The programming and customization landscape of Salesforce crystalizes around two primary concepts: *multitenant* and *declarative versus custom* strategies. The multitenant constraints color a lot of the customization technologies in an effort to protect the shared customer/user resources. In order to enable maximum functionality without risking performance, Salesforce surfaces "declarative" options for customization as much as possible. These declarative options are configurations from the web interface. Also known as "clicks not code," the strategy of providing configuration and automation options without allowing code access has gained wide appeal. This has aligned with the global movement of "low-code" solution building. Expect to see more capability enablement from Salesforce as the company invests in more easy-to-use and easy-to-build tools.

How to Discern Platform Capabilities

Why is the programming landscape important to architects? There is no perfect platform that can do every task fast, cheaply, and at scale. Those aspects are always variable, even if you are using the native or core functions of a platform out of the box. For each advertised capability of a cloud platform that you are evaluating, you need to understand what limits are placed on it. This is especially important if you are moving from on-premises capabilities or if you are looking to migrate to a platform from any other. Assuming that an advertised feature is unlimited or has perfect parity with any other platform can lead to problems. Any platform that allowed users to do "infinite" anything would get abused and overloaded.

As we try to determine the fit and capabilities of a new platform, we use a lot of extreme terms to find out where the boundaries are. If possible, we record the sessions to reference later. Sometimes salespeople can overdescribe functionality. Figure 8-1 lists some terms that you should use and watch for when trying to understand a capability.

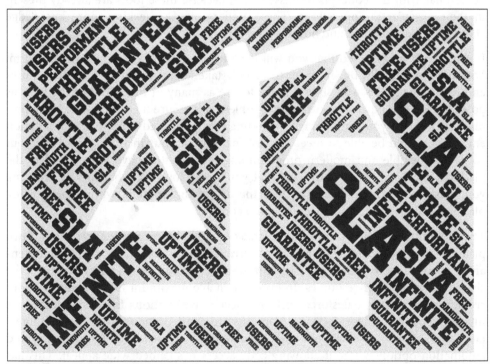

Figure 8-1. Finding a balance with extreme terms

Learn to see the balancing act between capability and capacity. Ask questions to find out the extent of the capability and possible implications of easy-to-overlook limitations:

- Is X unlimited?
- Is X never down?
- Is X free?
- Is X guaranteed?
- Is X instant?
- Is X throttled?
- Are there any extra licenses required?
- What does this let me replace?

These questions will help you figure out which functionality is specific to your purpose and which can be leveraged across an enterprise. When you look at customization options *and* you have a budget to manage, you examine whether you already have something that does X (or if you can replace X with Y). While you learn about the capabilities discussed in this section, like customization, automation, batch processing, data load, transactions, and web services, try to understand the ones that differentiate Salesforce from other platforms.

Customization Options and Limits

Figure 8-2 shows a layout of the main types of code used in the Salesforce platform. There are other varieties of programming and customization tools available that work in the other stacks, but we are focusing on core platform options here.

The first point to understand is that the programming that can be done on the Salesforce platform is *in addition to* the core stack program. You are able to add functionality, but you are not able to touch the existing platform code. You can alter some behavioral aspects of the system, where doing so has specifically been enabled. You can also modify the user experience to make it *seem* as though you have altered the way the platform works, even though this is not actually the case. From a computer science perspective, it's also important to know that the various languages you can use are all interpreted languages and not compiled into executable bytecode.

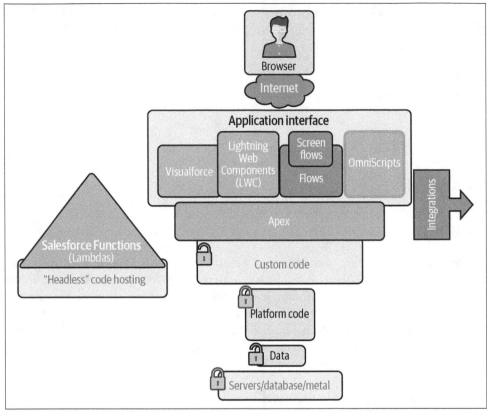

Figure 8-2. Types of code and where each type lives

There are several stages of bytecode that are maintained behind the scenes and refreshed when your scripts are updated or called by other backend processes. Administrators and developers do not have to deal with compiled code like JARs or gzipped files. In sum, there's a lot you can change in different places, but you can't change everything. This makes code promotion feel a bit like changing the tires on a moving car (when that car is a rental). That analogy should help you understand why so much time is spent on code management tools and not snapshots, backups, and recovery. Keep that in mind as we go over the various major toolsets in the customization space.

Limits are another factor that should always be kept in mind when it comes to customization in Salesforce. Every tool built on the Salesforce platform is subject to the I/O and CPU limits that keep the multitenant availability of the platform secure from slowdowns. Governor limits keep you from writing code that creates too much resource demand on the platform. How much is defined by many different qualifications. One limit is that you can only query the database so many times in a transaction, which in Salesforce is any chain of code functions started by a specific event. If an event calls code that calls other code that creates something that calls other code, that is all considered part of a single transaction. Transactions also have other limits, like memory size and execution time. Platform events and Salesforce functions are the first true exceptions to that rule; they run outside of the Salesforce transaction, effectively in a separate compute space. Salesforce Functions programming is still very new and not quite in vogue yet, but it should be *very* strongly considered for custom development in medium and large organizations.

Another limit to be aware of is the maximum number of lines of code. The limit is currently stated as 6 MB. Some types of code (e.g., comments) are excluded from this sum, but it is still important to be aware that this constraint exists. Hitting the maximum can require some tricky redesigns and cleanup activities.

Salesforce also sets a limit with regard to *code coverage*, which relates to writing unit test code to confirm that your Apex code functions as intended prior to promotion (we'll discuss this further in "Apex" on page 84). Production instances require that 75% of all lines of Apex code must be covered by test code. Letting your instance's code coverage hover near 75% can lead to chaotic attempts to improve your code coverage being blocked by code coverage errors. Staying comfortably above this threshold is a golden rule that can help you avoid disastrous consequences.

Coding Options

The rest of this chapter focuses on the different types of development platforms that exist inside the Salesforce platform. These code platforms are used for customization and automation.

Keep an eye on the following aspects when you are reviewing each of the platforms (I'll provide summary scores for all of them, based largely on my own experiences working with them, for purposes of comparison):

- DevOps maturity
- Language genealogy and popularity
- Usage applications
- Ease of use and learning

DevOps maturity refers to the ability to manage code with common tools like Git, Jenkins, Jira, and PMD. This score is based on the enterprise software management tools that can be used with each option discussed here (for simplicity's sake, from here on I'll refer to them all as "languages"). Mature organizations have heavy requirements for managing code. Regulation and compliance requirements also factor into many organizations' choices as table stakes, regardless of how new or shiny a technology is. More often than not, the rule is: "If it can't be governed (with our existing governance controls), we can't use it."

Language genealogy and popularity is a factor in how easy it is to find developers that are comfortable using a particular coding option. Apex, for example, is syntactically very similar to Java. Java developers will have a fairly low barrier of entry to learning Apex. Java is a very popular language, so this should provide a sense of security for those worried about stepping into a proprietary ecosystem.

Each of the languages described here has a specific set of capabilities that makes it better suited to some use cases than others. Knowing what each language is most often used for and comparing that to the type of development you are going to be doing will guide your level of investment in each. Some of these specific development focus areas might include pixel-perfect UI design, high-scale data synchronization, and citizen developer productivity.

In addition, some of the language types are based on commonly used formats or languages outside of Salesforce. Some of these languages have more unique components, which increases the learning curve required to achieve proficiency.

The final critical element to keep in mind is the difference between the language specification and the container that parses and executes the language. There are layers.

Apex

Apex is the foundational language of the core Salesforce platform. It's not the original language of Salesforce customization, but it is currently at the heart of all of the other languages in play within Salesforce. From a structure and syntax perspective, it is very similar to Enterprise JavaBeans and borrows heavily from the Java language specification. Classes are registered and called as needed, with varying states of compilation and bytecode. Apex is interpreted by a custom interpreter, not with the classic Java compiler, but there are only a few idiosyncrasies that a Java developer would need to figure out to get productive in Apex. Apex is referred to as the foundation of Salesforce because of its ability to interact with the data layers. The other tools discussed here either have limited data layer interaction or require Apex code to do data manipulation.

Apex runs with memory, CPU time, and data retrieval limitations referred to as *governor limits*. These limits prevent code from taking more than a small portion of the shared resources. Writing code that efficiently works within the boundaries proposed by each of these limitations is a special art. There's a lot of knowledge required to use the safe data retrieval functions that ensure that code isn't stopped due to running afoul of one of them. These underlying limits are applicable across all of the interactions with the Salesforce programming layers. Even the no-code systems have to play within these limits.

While almost all data is exposed with out-of-the-box web services, you can also build custom web services with Apex. Apex is the data broker behind all of the frontend programming systems, as well as allowing custom inbound interactions with other systems.

Another topic somewhat unique to Apex development is unit testing with test classes. *Test classes* are special pieces of code that you create to pass arguments to your Apex code to simulate the code being run (see Example 8-1). If a test class encounters an unhandled error condition, infinite loop, governor limit, type mismatch, or other compilation/execution error, the test will fail. As mentioned previously, the platform's test engine detects which lines of code are used ("covered") by the unit test scenarios of your test classes and tracks the percentage of lines covered. If your code contains a logical fork (if/else), there must be test functions that cover both paths to get 100% coverage. Salesforce sets a minimum threshold of 75% code coverage in total for a production org's codebase; if this threshold is not met, updates to your production code will not be allowed. These problems can be extremely difficult to resolve, so make sure any new developers are well trained in the best practices around test classes and not just basic Apex syntax.

Example 8-1. Apex code and test code coverage

```
CODE.cls
Public class MyClass{
      void MySpecialFunction(int myvalue){
            if(myvalue>1){
                  let x=y;   //Only covered by testFunction2
                  let a=b;   //Only covered by testFunction2
            }else{
                  let x=b;   //Only covered by testFunction1
                  let a=17;    //Only covered by testFunction1
            }
            for(i=0;i<1000;i++){
                  if(myvalue==1){
                      a=9000   //Only covered by testFunction1
                      break;   //Only covered by testFunction1
                  }else{
                      a=i;   //Only covered by testFunction2
                  }
            }
      }
}


TEST.cls
Public class MyClass_TEST{
```

```
@isTest
void testFunction1(){
        MyClass.MySpecialFunction(1); //passes a 1 to the Code
}
void testFunction2(){
        MyClass.MySpecialFunction(2); //passes a 2 to the Code
}
}
```

Apex can be developed and edited in three primary integrated development environments (IDEs): Visual Studio Code (VS Code), Salesforce Code Builder, and the Salesforce Developer Console. VS Code, Microsoft's language- and platform-agnostic development environment, has extensive plug-in support and a web-based repository integration. Code Builder is a fully featured web-based IDE, and the Developer Console is a more lightweight web-based editor.

Apex summary scores:

- DevOps maturity: 100%
- Language genealogy and popularity—Java/C++: 80%
- Usage applications: 85%
- Ease of use and learning: 45%

Visualforce

Visualforce (VF) is the Coldfusion or PHP of Salesforce. VF pages serve several functions within the platform. They're created as empty HTML pages, into which you can drop any standard HTML, CSS, and JavaScript. VF pages are limited to the HTML4 doctype, so you'll have to use Bootstrap to access any HTML5-specific features that you want to nest inside them. Fancy HTML and JavaScript isn't the main point of VF, though. VF pages support a tag-based language that is custom to Salesforce. The tags are basically templates and slots for standard data access and form functions. You can do quite a bit with VF customization with Apex extensions to user-created custom tags as well as "code behind" pages.

Although Lightning Web Components, which we'll look at shortly, is the recommended modern development toolset today for visual customization requirements, quick time to market and nimble functions like PDF rendering (one of my favorite uses for VF pages) have kept VF alive in the toolbelts of many Salesforce developers, and it remains a relevant tool today.

Visualforce summary scores:

- DevOps maturity: 90%
- Language genealogy and popularity—PHP (tag-based templates): 60%
- Usage applications: 65%
- Ease of use and learning: 55%

Aura

Aura was a huge step forward for Salesforce, embracing more of the capabilities of browser-based JavaScript over the server-side processing of VF. Aura could be written in the web-based Developer Console, but it required following certain patterns that were not aligned with the more open JavaScript patterns. This was one of the factors that led to slower adoption of this toolset. Aura attempted to enforce some JavaScript isolation security by passing all code through an interpreter. This had mixed results from a security perspective but did open the door for more JavaScript developers to enter the ecosystem and build rich components.

 Aura is sometimes referred to as Lightning Components, though that's actually a subset of the Aura framework. This is not to be confused with Lightning Web Components, discussed in the following section. The Lightning Experience (LEX) in Salesforce is not a programming framework, but a platform update representing a shift to a richer, single-page application design for Salesforce's pages. It's an upgraded user experience facelift for the entire platform. The former, more "static" page style is now referred to as "Classic." There are many organizations that are still living in the Classic Experience, due to heavy customizations that are tightly coupled to the Classic UI and framework rules. LEX changed the rules, mostly for the better, but there are some quibbles about performance and some changed capabilities. LEX is the underlying UI/server framework, but to confuse things further, the UI/CSS visual styles are separately referred to as the Salesforce Lightning Design System (SLDS).

Aura has effectively been marked for deprecation by Salesforce in favor of the newer Lightning Web Components. It does not have a lifecycle end date, though, and there have not been any major concerns voiced publicly (to date) that would steer one away from its continued use. There are cases for which open source Aura components are still very good choices for reuse, despite the technology having fallen slightly from favor.

Aura summary scores:

- DevOps maturity: 80%
- Language genealogy and popularity—JavaScript: 60%
- Usage applications: 65%
- Ease of use and learning: 55%

Lightning Web Components

Lightning Web Components (LWC) was a major step forward in standards-based rich application development. It enables the use of modern development and HTML features including HTML5, ECMAScript 12, and CSS3. Salesforce works closely with the web standards group that publishes updates to the language specification. New features and versions from this open specification are then fairly quickly added to the LWC feature set as well. This means that developers can not only use the latest functionality, but their experience in the language is modern and portable (can be used on other platforms). The LWC development framework also aligns closely with other JavaScript frameworks, like Node.js. Leaning into already established patterns and fast-tracking modern features has accelerated LWC's adoption by an army of fans and practitioners.

LWC is also the best option for customizing any mobile experience you are targeting. LWC components can be created display-aware and be customized to each display-type. For pixel-perfect designs on different devices, LWC is currently the only option. (Not enough information is available on the OmniStudio Mobile SDK yet for me to weigh it against LWC.) LWC customizations can be included in flows as well as other niche products. This is the go-to customization tool for everything that Salesforce has opened for development.

One of the future-proof, reading-between-the-lines directions that LWC is heading in has to do with trying to build web page components that have an enforceable security and permissions model. Each component only needs to be able to interact with its own data and not to gather data from any other parts of the page. So, the framework must prevent easy access to data each component is not supposed to be able to read. The ability to have multiple web components on the same screen with measured, secured, and limited access to other components is a bit of a holy grail for platforms. Being able to create an "app store" model of resellable components with security enforcement could possibly drive a new gold rush in enterprise web development. Watch for continued development that supports this secure component infrastructure. LWC, Lightning Locker (formerly Locker Service), and Lightning Web Security (LWS) are steps along this path.

Figure 8-3 shows some of the layers involved in LWC. Directionality depends on your perspective, as a consuming user or a developer. From the user's perspective, a request for a page starts in the browser. The Salesforce server responds by loading basic web page resources and the core LWC processing libraries. Those files are processed by the browser's JavaScript engine, which starts pulling other resources and orchestrating what will become the document object model (DOM). The browser will start rendering the page visually as the DOM is assembled. The HTML, CSS, and JavaScript files from LWC are passed to the LWC transpiler. You can think of the transpiler as a plug-in or an extension of the browser's standard JavaScript interpreter. The extension helps the code that is now running in the browser communicate with the Salesforce system. All of the LWC files and their data are then combined and presented in the browser. This is a highly simplified explanation of several systems processing and communicating in disjointed harmony.

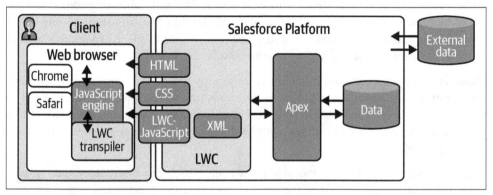

Figure 8-3. Examining the layers of LWC

LWC summary scores:

- DevOps maturity: 95%
- Language genealogy and popularity—JavaScript: 85%
- Usage applications: 100%
- Ease of use and learning: 80%

Flows

Flows are an exciting Salesforce feature that is growing in functionality and popularity every day. Unfortunately, there are several dozen popular tools out there with "flow" in the name, so we need to do some differentiating to make sure you know how to tell them apart. Salesforce's Flow Builder is a visual development tool with an easy-to-learn, point-and-click design surface. If diagramming in Visio, Lucid, Miro, or PowerPoint is familiar to you, building flows with this tool should be easy to pick up. The logical vocabulary is surprisingly simple; it feels more like learning what different traffic signs mean than learning a programming language. A flow is a series of steps and interactions that can do multiple things. Semantically, triggers, classes, and methods are the units of code that are written in Apex. Flows are flows. There are different types of flows that you can write with Flow Builder.

Flows can run with no user interaction, based on listening to data changes behind the scenes. They can also be launched from buttons and show multiple screens with logical forking between the screens. The screens are form-based and not meant to be designed pixel-perfect to a specification, though that is possible with extensions.

Besides being easy for developers to pick up, flows are easy for non-developers to read and understand. Done correctly, flows are almost self-documenting. The steps and the data dependencies can be organized visually, and with good naming conventions, errors are quickly resolved with built-in alerting and debugging tools. As your flows increase in complexity and criticality, you should obviously step up your discipline. Using reusable sub-flows as well as using formulas in place of logical branches will greatly improve the readability of your flows.

Flows have a handful of additional limitations compared to the more traditional Apex code, but for case-by-case automation and user interactions you shouldn't need to worry about these. There are step, record count, and memory allocation limits that you can hit once you get into more complex solutions, but the capabilities of flows are evolving rapidly.

Flows can be extended with Invocable Apex code, which can then return data or perform other functions outside of the flow. Flows can also be extended with Salesforce Functions (which have even fewer limitations than Apex code) in the same way. These two avenues make flows suitable for a highly scalable range of applications.

Flows summary scores:

- DevOps maturity: 70%
- Language genealogy and popularity—Visual flow charting: 90%
- Usage applications: 75%
- Ease of use and learning: 95%

Process Builder (Deprecated)

Process Builder was an even more simplified visual automation tool. Over the past few release years, all of the functionality that differentiated Process Builder processes from flows has migrated to flows. They're still around, but they have been marked for end-of-life support by Salesforce; as of summer 2023, you can no longer create new ones. It's unclear when they might be fully disabled, so if you are inheriting an org with preexisting Process Builder processes, you need to know what they are and how dependent you are on them as a sunsetting technology.

Process Builders summary scores:

- DevOps maturity: 70%
- Language genealogy and popularity—Wizard-like: 75%
- Usage applications: 65%
- Ease of use and learning: 100%

Workflow Rules (Deprecated)

Workflow Rules are hard to distinguish verbally from flows, which are also a type of workflow tool. However, they're not as visually friendly as flows or Process Builder processes. Workflow Rules—sometimes referred to simply as "Workflows," though that's actually a less apt descriptor—are sets of actions and steps with a very limited amount of logic that you enter into a form page. They are almost single units of logic with no complexity. They include a lot of "if X then do Y" rules, but not a whole lot of "else" extensions beyond that.

Workflow Rules is on a similar deprecation timeline as Process Builder, so the same sunset rules apply (as of winter 2023, you can no longer create new Workflow Rules). The path forward is just to make flows as simple or complex as you need them. The consolidation of automation types is a great cleanup and simplification step. Again, just be aware of your organization's dependence on a dead-end technology.

Workflow Rules summary scores:

- DevOps maturity: 90%
- Language genealogy and popularity—Form-based rules: 20%
- Usage applications: 65%
- Ease of use and learning: 55%

Salesforce Functions

Salesforce Functions is actually an integration to another behind-the-scenes platform that can do explosive work compared to in-platform code. Salesforce Functions can be written in Java, JavaScript, or TypeScript. The code is run in a separate processing system without any of the governors or limits imposed by in-platform code. The new environment's security is so tightly integrated into the Salesforce platform that only a few additional steps are involved in making use of this new scalable platform addition.

Since this new application hosting environment supports Java, TypeScript, and Java-Script, a wealth of open source shared libraries are available to plug and play quickly as Salesforce Functions. Libraries for amortization tables, image manipulation, and other binary file creation routines that have already been created can be leveraged with ease. It also increases your available developer resource pool to experienced wielders of these other nonproprietary languages.

Salesforce Functions is an additional license cost, but it can unshackle your development goals and help transform Salesforce into a full-powered application development platform. It brings scalable compute, unlimited data processing, and free component reuse into the platform. As an architect, this is one of the more drastic changes to the ability of the Salesforce platform to solve enterprise problems. Forecasting your need for highly scalable workloads and investing early in the proper technology is a key architect's goal, and this will be a critical forward-looking capability to consider.

The reception of Salesforce Functions has been mixed, however. It is very likely that advancements in many expansive technologies like this will be cooled or paused during market downturns. There may be a move to re-create this functionality inside of Heroku. Salesforce's position on AWS integrations also seems to have pivoted, which may make direct competition with AWS Lambda something the company steers away from.

Salesforce Functions summary scores:

- DevOps maturity: 95%
- Language genealogy and popularity—Java, JavaScript, and TypeScript: 100%
- Usage applications: 35%
- Ease of use and learning: 70%

Package Development and Use

Salesforce has its own application marketplace, called the AppExchange (*https://oreil.ly/dBtlY*). Businesses that enter into a partner relationship can host and sell solutions on the AppExchange. When you purchase one of them, you are permitted to install a "package" into your org based on a per-organization or per-user licensing model. Packages can contain a wide range of components, from a single Lightning component to a full application with custom classes, record types, screens, flows, and external connections.

There are two primary types of packages: *managed*, which must comply with a set of established code and security requirements for public distribution, and *unmanaged*, which are designed for internal deployment within your own org. All managed packages listed on the AppExchange must pass a rigorous set of security checks before they can be published. Unmanaged packages do not require review. They are typically used for customizations that benefit from self-contained, version-controlled lifecycle management (such as pages and record types that depend on each other and should be deployed and upgraded as a single unit). They can also be used to freely share code in an open source style.

Managed packages are not editable by the consumer. Only the publisher can modify the code. In effect, they are commercial off-the-shelf plug-ins provided by a vendor, even if there is no cost to acquire or use them. There are many free packages available on the AppExchange, often created by community contributors who wish to share their customizations with other Salesforce users. In contrast, unmanaged packages offer greater control to the end user and are easier to modify, update, and customize. It is worth noting that unmanaged packages can be shared between orgs, but there is no official structure to distribute or manage them—if you use an unmanaged package in your org that you did not develop, then you assume the risk of any bugs or failures, just as if you had developed the package yourself.

Packages can use any supported authorization technique necessary, from the internal Salesforce permission model and role inheritance to external connections to APIs or web services. It is even possible to expose web service endpoints within a package that extend the external accessibility of the Salesforce org in which it is deployed. External connections, whether outbound from an org to a service or inbound from an external entity to an org, are typically secured with either a predetermined private key (commonly known as an API key) or a standardized token exchange mechanism known as OAuth (see Chapter 5).

The Good

With the adoption of VS Code as the primary developer tool for most Salesforce custom code (Apex and LWC), the developer experience is on par with most other platforms. Moving code from developer systems through staging to production systems is quite straightforward, and there's enough flexibility to support a range of development patterns to match any existing business processes. Apex is a mature language, and Salesforce regularly releases new functionality and quality-of-life improvements to the stack.

Flows are another game changer. They allow a much faster onboarding pathway to automation development for potential builders that are bored by, or just don't take to, "code." As demand for new developers rises, this will be critical. New talent pools will open up, and it will allow the transitioning of people with other skill sets into high-demand areas of programming and automation.

Flows are not limited to working only with Salesforce data and structures; they are able to call out and interact with other systems as well. The acquisition of MuleSoft leads me to believe that this is an area that will continue to mature and gain in power. Being effectively self-documenting and somewhat less apt at hiding bad practices or nefarious goals, flows can potentially speed time to market for the vast majority of technical endeavors.

The Gotchas

Developing in Salesforce carries a few caveats. In the syntax, there are a handful of unique structures to the language that must be learned. This is always the case with a new platform/language, so this should be expected. Java and other C-type mavens will have very little trouble adapting to the syntax. Additionally, there are some configuration-level features that your potential developers should become acquainted with before starting to write code. Not being aware that an out-of-the-box feature exists can lead to developers wasting tons of time and creating unnecessary technical debt. Teach them to assume that everything has already been done before and to only code new features if they're absolutely positive they aren't available.

The Salesforce development landscape can be a moving target. With shifts in direction and security concerns, some components can change or even lose support entirely on very short timelines. (Frameworks like Aura and Salesforce Functions have gone from hero to zero in record time. These changes are rare, but they do happen.) Salesforce usually softens any landings if you have committed to something that has changed—this is one of the most engaged customer success companies I have ever worked with.

The next major hurdle for transitioning development practices into Salesforce is code management at scale. Namespaces are implemented, but only very superficially. They don't offer much in the way of grouping or managing code or system resources. There's not even a concept of folders for organizing sets of code. As such, a file naming convention is critical for teams working with large codebases or many teams. There are several search tools for finding where elements are used across the ecosystem, but these are no substitute for legitimate code organization.

The biggest headache that developers will encounter is learning how and when to work with governor limits. Operations that touch data have to be specifically engineered to do so safely, from their inception. The old model of "build it and tune it if it breaks" is not an option. You get errors if you write code that matches a pattern that even has the potential to perform poorly. This is Salesforce protecting you not only from your own bad code but, more importantly, from the bad code of others. It means there's an extra set of meta-models to keep in your brain of what you can and can't do.

With on-premises or consumption-based cloud systems, you have control over your resource usage; you have the option to buy more hardware or pay for a higher tier, respectively. Salesforce is a managed platform; you have limits, and many of them you cannot buy your way around. It's much more akin to writing C code with memory management or writing code for microcontroller/system-on-chip (SOC) systems. It is vital to understand the size of the breadbox before trying to move into it.

The Growth

The development capabilities of the platform are expanding rapidly and growing with each new acquisition. Figure 8-4 shows some of the directional goals within the ecosystem. It's gaining features that appeal to non-developers with low-code options. Salesforce is also adopting frameworks that allow for reuse of existing skills without having to bank on the longevity or value of learning a proprietary language.

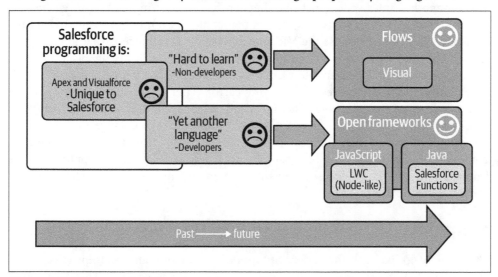

Figure 8-4. Directional shift: easier to learn and more open to developers from other frameworks

The expansion of the Salesforce core platform from a development capabilities perspective has had a clear focus on allowing huge groups of non-Salesforce developers to find an easy way into the ecosystem. This has balanced the market cost of Salesforce talent while greatly increasing the size of the talent pool. This helps ensure that the resource market changes don't impact your investment as much as they could in a proprietary skills model.

The AppExchange is also growing, along with the levels of ease and trust the platform supports. Watch for continued overhauls of the development plumbing that supports shareable components. Once there's a potential for profit at scale with smaller investments, developers will rush into the space. That rush will provide you with more and more power to serve your business and enable you to quickly pivot to new opportunities. For now, there's still a tick/tock progression with capability, then security. Salesforce will probably move incrementally toward this goal, which will seed fervor in the developer market with only moderate return for itself.

 "Tick/tock" is a moniker for a pattern of technological progress made popular by Intel in chip microarchitecture, where chip models are designated as either a *tick* (an improvement in efficiency or die optimization) or a *tock* (a new set of capabilities or features that have not been implemented before). I'm making this analogy in relation to the software pattern of "make something new" then "secure and optimize it."

There's another intersection that may happen before the AppExchange reaches the maximum developer attractiveness model that could disrupt the market: virtual reality (VR). This is not because the VR marketplace or experience is that amazing; it's due to the fact that much of the current VR innovation is taking place on very mature, secure, and monetizable platforms. Habits die hard, and being willing to swap infrastructures requires a very shiny carrot. There were 64-bit platforms that could overpower the aging x86 systems for full decades, but they didn't gain adoption until providers removed all the rough edges. Similarly, the resistance to doing work on mobile devices lasted for years, until the interface turned a corner; then we couldn't port functions to mobile fast enough. That user experience tipping point is important to watch for, because it can sneak up on you and disrupt all your plans and force itself into your patterns.

Summary

There's a lot to like with the variety of types of automation and customization available in the Salesforce platform. It is not unlimited in any context. That being said, very few orgs reach a limit on their ability to execute on the platform. Salesforce is usually earmarked for specific functionality or lines of business. This is a good model to adopt to grow into your stake in Salesforce, but it's also very possible to jump in with both feet. The customization options are there to do whatever you need to do from an application space. Working with some of the acquisitions and stacks, like Heroku, Tableau, and MuleSoft, requires different investments in talent. Staying within the Salesforce-owned stacks offers increased seamlessness, but integrations with other systems work quite well too. It's often a toss-up whether an in-ecosystem offering is the best of breed or close enough to the current best to pick for the added convenience of a single relationship.

Salesforce has pushed the LWC development stack hard, and it's a strong move. LWC is an easier transition for developers coming from other ubiquitous stacks like Node.js, React, Vue, and other JavaScript-based platforms. This greatly opened the resource market for luring in developers, as well as making it possible to reuse more Stack Exchange code from other adjacent platforms. This move stabilized the salary requirements for Salesforce developers, as the frenzy around the platform increased. Apex is still the foundation of data access and data modeling, and the core of any extended customization effort, so it shouldn't be de-emphasized when you're building teams. In addition, Salesforce performance and security are still primarily managed in Apex, and that should tell you all you need to know for your goals in building teams and expertise.

Salesforce Functions could change the landscape significantly, but that future is still on the horizon. There should be some good showcase projects with Salesforce Functions soon that will help convince more customers to use them to expand the power of the extended Salesforce ecosystem. The biggest use cases for Salesforce Functions will likely be in large enterprise implementations. Small and medium implementations will likely be very happy with the capabilities of the core programming and customization offerings described in this chapter.

CHAPTER 9

Mobile Platforms and Customization

Salesforce offers several different options for mobile device application functionality. When contemplating your options for mobile, take care to gather a full perspective on the capabilities of each. Names and features in this space are highly fluid. In addition, Salesforce's investment in the mobile landscape changes from year to year, and new platform offerings and acquisitions alter the momentum behind each stack. Salesforce isn't much different from other platforms trying to navigate the rapidly changing mobile technology landscape in these regards.

To navigate the options available, it's important to understand the different types of mobile applications. For the purposes of this book, we're going to group them into three categories: web-based, native, and hybrid. These distinctions are important for security and fit for each use case they serve. Some offer highly customizable, independent interfaces while others are prebuilt and only partially customizable. Compatibility, functionality, and capabilities also vary across platforms (iOS or Android) and device types. It is therefore crucial to have a clear device roadmap solidified before starting any major Salesforce implementation that includes mobile device access.

Mobile Application Types

At a high level, we can distinguish between three types of mobile applications: native, hybrid, and web. Web-based applications have code and functionality available on the internet and displayed in the very open standard of HTML. Every browser application is supposed to conform to the standards of what each element has been defined to serve. Web applications all create functionality in the same way. It is no coincidence that when you are viewing websites on different devices with different browsers (e.g., Edge, Chrome, Safari, Firefox, and Opera), the pages mostly look the same. Some web app frameworks, like Salesforce, can be optimized for different screen sizes and devices, but only to a certain extent. Native mobile applications can be either more or less restrictive than web applications; the key point with this type is that they require more effort to customize, with the benefit of being fully customizable. Salesforce has tools available to create all of these variants:

- Web applications that can be almost fully customized (within the context of web controls)
- Native applications that offer very few customization options
- Native applications that offer moderate customization options
- Hybrid applications wrapped in native shells that are highly customizable (within the context of web controls)
- Native applications that are highly customizable

Web applications can be built with many different underlying languages, but the HTML output that is sent to us when we open a URL in our browser is mostly the same. Forcing the many hardware and platform providers to all start speaking a single common language was one of the things that drove the explosion of the web: we finally could access many systems with a small set of applications installed on our devices. It became very gauche to require custom software (not a web browser) to access your application. Adopting this new open standard for receiving information from the internet reduced the burden on users to keep up with interfaces for each company's data. Ease of consumption won out over proprietary delivery.

After the web took off, malicious websites started to become something we had to worry about. Browsers had to sacrifice more and more functionality to make sure that critical systems on the client side couldn't be attacked. The web browser is supposed to be a simple window through which we are viewing web content. The innovation of web technologies had to keep pace with bad actors that were turning up. Web browsers have a very limited set of operations that they can perform on a user's device. Grabbing GPS location information is allowed, but only with permissions. Reading from the device storage or hard drive is not allowed. Turning the device on or off is *definitely* not allowed. Web page code is also not supposed to be able to perform other types of on-device functions, like "read my personal files," "turn on my camera," "send something to my printer," and "read my fingerprint." Many of these things are still possible via websites, but layers of security exist to ensure you are in control of when and how they happen.

Ninety-five percent of web applications live on a server in a building that could be anywhere. The other five percent are pulled across the internet and appear in your browser. You are looking at the intentional output of the application server to your device's browser. Any heavy lifting, like data storage or building a custom PDF, is done on the server side. The actual code that does the heavy lifting is executed on the server, and your browser is only sent the resulting file. (That said, offloading server work to a browser is a common pattern these days; some of these heavy lifting functions *can* move to the browser.)

Native mobile applications are primarily built the other way around with regard to the code. Most of the code lives on your device; the data, if any, is pulled from servers over the internet. There is still lots of code on remote servers, but the code that you are interacting with is running on your device (at least, more so than with web applications). Code created for mobile devices has generally been built with a bit more trust and better cooperation with the physical hardware functionality of your device.

With the added trust and features of native mobile applications, a native application can get access to and listen for actions coming from another application. An example is when an authentication code is sent from an application to your SMS text message account for your phone. Native apps can be given permission to watch your SMS application and read the data in the messages themselves. This process would be almost impossible to implement with a web application, although capabilities are growing for these apps to have more device access safely. Currently, native applications still have the advantage when it comes to direct and trustable integration directly with hardware features.

The final advantage of native applications is being able to cater to very specific screen sizes, like smart watches and rings, cash registers, and handheld scanners. Web applications assume a certain minimum size and shape. The majority of the various smart devices in use today are simply not able to easily take advantage of the niceties of HTML and web pages: the screens are too small to offer a reusable experience, and battery and power limitations that also impact processing power figure into the experience as well.

Hybrid applications attempt to get the best of both worlds by having a native application "shell" and also being able to pull in and reuse web content. They still have to be installed from an appropriate app store, but hybrid apps can implement fully custom native controls as well as displaying custom web content. The amount of custom code you need to write can be reduced if existing web pages can be brought in to use and interact with the native component shell. A hybrid app is basically an enhanced and customizable web browser, locked to process content according to your rules. As long as those rules are similar to regular rules for web applications, you can make use of a single code base to serve both types. Designing something that can possibly work for both purposes is hard—you have to build a discipline for managing multiuse code— but it's almost always worth the effort to avoid having two entirely separate code bases to maintain.

Figure 9-1 provides a very high-level illustration of the difference between the three types of mobile applications and where the bulk of the code lives in each type. While a hybrid approach provides the most flexibility, the trade-off is managing more than one code base for display functionality.

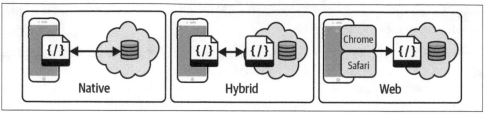

Figure 9-1. Native versus hybrid versus web apps on mobile

Salesforce Mobile App

The Salesforce mobile app, formerly known as the Salesforce1 app, is one of several native applications in the Salesforce ecosystem. This native app is designed to surface Salesforce application data to the licensed internal users of your Salesforce org. (Serving content to customers or external users is covered in the next section.) The app is capable of displaying all of the major types of data from the web application. It is very useful for working in standard ways with standard requirements within a modern utility application. It's perfect for people working with Salesforce data on a day-to-day basis. The Salesforce mobile app is mostly a native mobile app with some ability to frame in content written for the web. If you create custom data for people to use and manage, you will not need to worry about the differentiation between the web application and the native mobile application. The mobile app is available for no additional license cost and is an effective analog to the web interface.

The mobile application can present challenges, however, for requirements that are not easily expressed in standard Salesforce data fields and actions. The freedom of design you have with web pages does not translate into the standard Salesforce mobile app; you do not have the control to make it look *exactly* like you may have envisioned. The mobile app checks the box of "build once, deploy twice," but if you want to go truly custom and details matter, you will be building once for desktop web and once more for mobile. Salesforce's mobile app is designed with the usability needs of daily users in mind. Other use cases should consider other options.

 From a user experience (UX) perspective, you'll typically want to build highly custom interfaces for two reasons: to entice users into interacting with your application or to make a complicated process easier to understand. Increasing appeal or clarity usually involves reducing information density. The Salesforce mobile app keeps to a very specific information density that is good for users who have a strong motivation to use the tool and/or are already familiar with the tool. (The more familiar you are with something, the more information density or noise you can tolerate.)

While most consumer tablets can run the exact same applications as their smaller-screen siblings, Salesforce has also created a mobile app variant exclusively for tablets. The tablet version of the mobile app has a few key differences and additional features, compared to the standard mobile app. For example, there are more customizable landing pages and increased flexibility with regard to content in page layouts. On the whole, it's a slightly more customizable experience. The tablet version is available on all current iPads, including the iPad mini. If mobile usage is your target, make sure you look at both options.

Salesforce Mobile Publisher

The Salesforce Mobile Publisher tool allows you to transform your Experience Cloud (Community) sites into branded, instantly deployable mobile applications. Whereas the Salesforce mobile app is intended for your employees and coworkers, the apps created with the Mobile Publisher are for your customers or external users. Any browser can access your Community sites, but the Mobile Publisher packages them as downloadable applications, available via Google Play and Apple's App Store. You can give each application a custom icon and name. There are many popular brand loyalty apps in the app marketplaces that are Mobile Publisher apps behind the scenes. Salesforce manages most of the lengthy security and review processes for you (though some circumstances may require some interaction), so there's no need to hire a mobile app technology team to manage or deploy your customer interaction portal mobile app. Your new mobile application is updated every time you update your community data or the Mobile Publisher layouts that reflect your Community site.

Salesforce Field Service

Salesforce Field Service (formerly Field Service Lightning) is a native mobile app tied to a specific license for Salesforce. It is focused on service tickets and technician routing, and it adds some features to the web-based interface. If you are considering Service Cloud as a part of your implementation, make sure you explore this app, which brings ticket and case management functionality and other platform features to your licensed users. (Remember, most "Clouds" are just additional functionality on your platform instance.) The Field Service app is based on the React.js framework but is not currently open for editing or customization directly. It supports LWC component additions, but does not alter the rest of the application itself (LWC components are displayed as items in a container; they cannot alter the container). React is a modern framework, so compared to other native applications you may have used, Field Service will likely look newer and have support for more features.

The Good

Salesforce continues to invest in mobile technologies according to demand and popularity. The divide between curated customer experiences and data-driven, one-size-fits-all employee experiences will likely continue to deepen. Devices and experiences will continue to be shaped by acquisitions of tools customized to more specific use cases. Look for additional offerings to come out of Salesforce for specific functionality around health care and financial services, two areas that are seeing huge growth in adoption of the Salesforce platform. All of the out-of-the-box offerings can immediately be used to add capabilities to your organization.

The Gotchas

Customizable mobile applications and *custom* mobile applications are two very different things. Deploying anything beyond the out-of-the-box experience can require exponentially more investment. If you are moving into the Salesforce space and are not already invested in mobile application development, don't expect Salesforce to be a silver bullet. There are many hidden skills that must be hard-won to start delivering custom mobile applications to your end consumers. Delivering to employees is easier because you can specify a consistent device, hardware, and security profile. Adding complications like VPNs and support for devices made by different manufacturers with different-sized screens and a variety of versions and carriers can exponentially multiply the effort and resources required to get functionality to consumers. Factor in product updates and add-ons that are not perfectly integrated with the mobile view, and you can end up on a long and painful path.

One of the trends to watch in the mobile space is adapting to the support costs involved with the Android operating system. Since Android is free and open source, every manufacturer is allowed to alter the operating system to suit their purposes. Each of these variations can cause app developers more effort to accommodate them. This problem is not limited to Salesforce by any stretch; it's known in the industry as "Android fracturing." The result is that "bring your own device" (BYOD) strategies carry the unintended consequence of a support penalty. Salesforce has acknowledged this by limiting its Android support to Samsung only. This should only impact you in the long term as Samsung and Apple device prices grow with reduced competition.

The Growth

Worldwide innovation in mobile development has slowed since the start of the pandemic. As regular work patterns resume, we should see more acquisitions and integrations supporting mobile devices. Behind the scenes, there have been many powerful integrations with omni-channel communications tools. Salesforce's Omni-Channel feature reaches your users where they are, mobile or desktop, in the channel apps that many are using, like Facebook Messenger or SMS messaging systems. Investing in mobile communications over mobile apps may speak better to the next generation of digital consumers. Providers will want to watch and adapt to the online communication style of more adaptive younger users. This generation of users will likely stick largely to the current, proven channels, but you should always be ready to follow your users if that changes.

In addition, as mentioned in the previous chapter, VR is finally on the horizon. There are pending versions of VR hardware that may be able to get over the weight, look, and safety hurdles currently keeping VR out of the mainstream. In 2018, I demoed the first WebGL/Aframe.io integration with Salesforce at Dreamforce. Aframe.io is a lightweight JavaScript library that simplifies some of the native WebGL JavaScript library's functionality. These libraries are a bridge to allow for VR experiences to be expressed in web pages—so, with the right application of JavaScript, your Salesforce site could be available in VR. There have been other, more official VR applications and proofs-of-concept since then, with other platforms and frameworks. The technology to bring existing software into VR already exists. The hardware just needs another solid improvement to hasten adoption.

Summary

Implementing Salesforce is an easy win on multiple fronts with regard to delivering mobile functionality on varying screen sizes. Salesforce provides turnkey mobile solutions that suit a wide range of use cases. If you think you will need a completely custom solution, go full custom off-platform. If your business can accept a "very good" experience, you will find many easy opportunities to achieve that with a fraction of the investment in custom mobile app frameworks, processes, and skills. The mobile landscape is currently changing slowly, but advancements are unpredictable. Keep your strategies flexible and loosely coupled to be able to absorb and adapt to changes.

CHAPTER 10

DevOps Systems and Patterns

On top of the components inside of the Salesforce ecosystem, there are a lot of additional tools that are commonly used by Salesforce practitioners. Figure 10-1 lists a few of the terms and systems that you may need to become familiar with to build a modern Salesforce DevOps practice. There are some offshoots of several of the open source tools with different names. They will vary a bit from platform to platform, and the idiosyncrasies with Salesforce's particular code management technologies require some understanding.

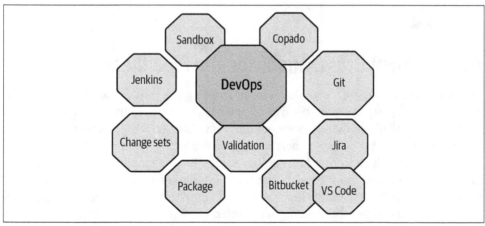

Figure 10-1. Elements of a Salesforce DevOps project

If you are already familiar with some of these tools and/or a certain way of doing things, you need to understand each of them can be used in a variety of different ways. If you move to a different organization, you may need to learn to use tools you have experience with in a different way than you are used to. Knowing how to describe the capabilities of the tools and systems you are familiar with and compare them to those used in your new environment will help you get up to speed faster. I have yet to work with two companies that execute DevOps in the exact same way. The most similarities are often observed between companies that have only recently started using Salesforce.

The most basic pattern in DevOps is *developer to consumer (user)*. Starting from that perspective, we will look into the different pathways and tools involved in moving Salesforce code and changes from the developer to the consumer. It's important to note that some of the pathways are slightly different depending on whether you are doing development on a company organization or building packages for distribution. We will start with the concepts involved with direct development and then go over the differences. This won't be a deep dive into DevOps processes—I'll only go deep enough to introduce the concepts, systems, and components that you will likely encounter.

Note that it's rare for a Salesforce implementation not to include at least three additional "companion" implementations to enable working with mature management tools. Expect to consider (hosted) Jira, GitHub/Bitbucket, and Jenkins. (While not directly related to DevOps, federated and two-factor/multifactor identity providers should also be on that list [e.g., Ping, Okta, and Azure AD].)

 DevOps is a more modern term for the evolved body of processes, which I learned to call *configuration management*. I tend to use the names interchangeably.

Development Orgs (Sandboxes and Pipelines)

When you start working with Salesforce, you are given a production instance. This is your production org. As mentioned in Chapter 1, you can spin up copies of your production org, called *sandboxes*, to try out different changes, write code or automation, test integrations, and get an understanding of the user experience. A sandbox is a copy of your production org, but sandboxes are also independent orgs of their own (and may be referred to as "orgs" rather than "sandboxes"). Sandboxes can be cloned from other sandboxes, but Salesforce orgs do not track their own lineage. Once created, they are all just sandbox orgs connected to your production org.

You can set up different tiers of sandbox orgs, depending on your needs and licensing, with different capabilities. (The biggest difference in org types is how much data they can hold.) You can then logically arrange these orgs into pipelines. (A *pipeline* is a logical progression pathway through a development cycle: *dev→test→production*.) Each sandbox gets its own URL, and different parts of the parent production org—or the entire org—are copied into it. There are some default user access changes that happen between copies to manage security, but we won't go into detail on that here; just be aware that the org creation/copying process can be adjusted and scripted.

Mapping, charting, and managing the logical pipelines, access to, and functions for each sandbox requires discipline and oversight in order to keep complicated or sensitive systems compliant. Figure 10-2 shows a representation of a rudimentary pipeline that might be set up for corporate development. Sandboxes are generally persistent but are refreshed on a regular basis. Changes are promoted up and down to keep the sandboxes in sync with approved updates. This process lends itself better to full regression testing but requires more care and feeding to maintain the state of each tier.

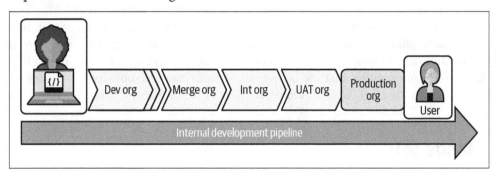

Figure 10-2. A typical internal publishing pipeline process

Figure 10-3 is a contrasting layout of a package development pipeline flow. *Scratch orgs* are temporary, time-limited development orgs. They are used more often in package development than persistent developer sandboxes (dev orgs). Scratch orgs are rapidly spun up and then destroyed based on a template definition for very explicit scenario testing.

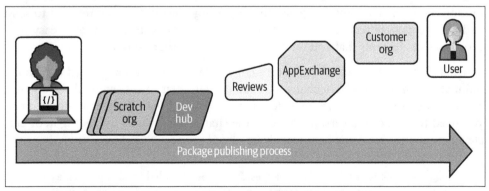

Figure 10-3. A typical independent software vendor package development process

Metadata

Metadata is another term that is a little misused in the Salesforce vocabulary. Though in other contexts it's generally taken to mean "data about data," the simplest descriptive definition in the context of Salesforce is "anything that is not record data." All of your code, configuration, setup, automations, labels, layouts, and pages are considered metadata. If you are editing code, you are editing metadata. If you create a new field on an object, that configuration is stored as metadata. If you store something in that field, however, that is not metadata; it's just data.

Configuration details about any changes to a Salesforce org are stored as XML. This XML metadata can be versioned and transferred between different development, test, and production orgs. "Metadata" is used mostly as an umbrella term to cover any of the configuration changes you make (code or clicks). There are very few pieces of a Salesforce configuration that are not stored in metadata and movable from instance to instance in different "bundle" concepts. Most of Salesforce's metadata is exposed in the web interface, but some can only be accessed by special tools.

Change Sets

Salesforce's built-in change management system is called *Changesets* (sometimes written *Change Sets*). As the name suggests, a change set is a named group of elements in your org that you have changed that you want to push to another sandbox or your production org. Change sets are a very capable configuration management tool for small teams. However, they break down when you have multiple teams or disparate teams that aren't in constant contact.

In each of your sandbox orgs, you can specify a "connection" to other orgs as a promotion pathway. The source org and the target org must both be configured to send and receive change sets independently. Once they're connected, it's a fairly easy process to select elements that you want to promote to another sandbox.

When a change set is created, it creates a copy of each element that's added to it, at the point at which it's added. All changes to that element that have been made by anyone, not just the current user, are included. If you make further changes to an element, you need to replace the version stored in the change set prior to uploading it, or create a new change set if you have already uploaded the previous change set.

Some configuration changes cannot be included in change sets, as they cannot be expressed in metadata/XML (yet). There are a small number of important changes that will have to be executed by an administrator directly on the org you wish to change. There are also some changes that cannot be cleanly undone. It's very important to be familiar with these elements during your change process.

DevOps Center

Salesforce has recently added new core functionality to the platform called *DevOps Center* that is intended to mature the operational capability of change management without requiring the use of external tools. This new product aims to add process management to the change set functionality. DevOps Center is entirely native to the Salesforce platform and free. There may be add-on paid features that roll out later, but the majority of the functionality should continue to be included as part of the base platform. Like Changesets, it is completely web interface-driven; no code, no scripts.

Validation and Test Code Coverage

When new metadata is promoted to a Salesforce org, the system runs validation checks to make sure that the changes don't reference anything that isn't available on or compatible with the target org. It also checks that the updates don't violate the standards for test code coverage. After validation has passed, you can choose whether or not to deploy. This step is part of every type of code promotion. The more complex your deployment pipeline is, the more complicated validation can be.

 The validation process described here is not to be confused with Validation Rules. Validation Rules are a data management function that controls what rules an entry has to follow to be allowed as input in a field. Sample Validation Rules include formats for email addresses and phone numbers, though Validation Rules allow for much more complex restrictions on data entry than those examples suggest.

We talked about test coverage in Chapter 8, but it's important to revisit it here. While technically a part of development and programming, writing unit tests is enforced in the validation and DevOps processes. Falling below the minimum threshold of 75% code coverage with unit tests can block code from being promoted or updated. The result of this can be a complete shutdown of your development pipeline, including halting many types of emergency fixes. The scoring system that calculates your current code coverage can also be accidentally cleared, and starting from zero can bring its own complications. Discipline is needed to manage this process if you are in an active environment.

Integrated Development Environments

As mentioned in Chapter 8, Salesforce's recommended IDE for working with code is VS Code. VS Code is a lighter-weight version of Microsoft's Visual Studio IDE that is centered around development on the .NET platform; it's platform-agnostic and supports almost every major programming language. Eclipse is another IDE that is popular among developers, primarily in Java-based languages. Eclipse is still used for MuleSoft development, but that is also migrating to VS Code. (MuleSoft is a Salesforce-acquired platform that enables custom integration and API orchestration.) PyCharm is a popular IDE used for Python development, and Intellij is another popular IDE that still has many users in the Salesforce ecosystem. Illuminated Cloud also has a faithful following among Salesforce developers as a very feature-rich IDE with a lot of Salesforce-specific functionality.

Apex, Aura, and VF can be edited with VS Code or the Developer Console, the browser-based IDE included in the core platform. The Developer Console is very lightweight and usable on any device that can browse the web. However, it does not support all of the plug-ins and DevOps automation that are available with VS Code and other more fully featured desktop IDEs. Working with LWC also requires an external editor; it's not currently possible to view and edit LWC code in the Developer Console.

Source Code Management Tools

There are many types of source code management tools that can be used with Salesforce. Most of the usual suspects that are popular in other ecosystems are compatible with Salesforce, to varying degrees. Git is the most common source code repository that I have seen in my engagements. Cloud-hosted versions of Git, like GitHub and Bitbucket, are commonly paired with Salesforce implementations to avoid working through firewalls and security to integrate with locally installed versions of source control and code management tools.

Salesforce upgrades its platform regularly to support the most modern security and integration standards. Other cloud services also keep that same pace with updates. Most of the time this means that cloud-to-cloud integrations between modern top-tier platforms are quick and well supported. On-premises systems may not have been kept up to the latest standards, which can lead to challenges when integrating more modern platforms with older ones. Source systems are subject to this same lag friction.

Project and Team Management Tools

Jira and Azure DevOps, from Atlassian and Microsoft, respectively, are the project management tools that are most commonly used by Salesforce development teams. They are both full-featured work management suites. This is where you hear about *epics*, *features*, *stories*, and *tasks* as the organizational units of development. Source code control information can be referenced passively in text or actively linked into these tools with integrations. For example, Copado can watch for a change in Jira and initiate a merge process in Git. Build and deployment processes can also be initiated by features or plug-ins with these tools.

Orchestration Tools

Orchestration, automation, and continuous integration and continuous delivery/ continuous deployment (CI/CD) tools function to move bundles of changes or code from one environment to another. These tools can include testing, validation, and vulnerability scanning, among other functions. There are many standalone options as well as service- and subscription-based tools that cover a wide range of DevOps functionality. Among these, there are a few automation tools that I see repeatedly used for pipeline management orchestration (probably due more to cost than functionality). Jenkins is the most common automation tool that I see implemented. It's an open source offering, which allows for it to be implemented relatively cheaply. Jenkins is also frequently at the core, or at least a component, of other orchestration toolsets and premium offerings.

Providers like Copado, Flosum, AutoRABIT, and Gearset have also incorporated various automation and CI/CD functions into hosted service offerings. These providers blur the distinctions between all of the individual toolsets and their components, providing an end-to-end service. The cloud-hosted service integrations work best with other best-of-breed cloud-hosted systems, for the same reasons discussed previously with regard to integrating systems with different levels of maturity.

Vulnerability Checking and Code Compliance Tools

Vulnerability checking and code compliance tools are relative newcomers, but they frequently appear in the Salesforce implementation and maintenance operations. PMD, CodeScan, AppOmni, and DigitSec have offerings that review source code and changes for vulnerabilities. These tools have different strengths and features, and can work at different points in the DevOps pipeline. Some of them have plug-ins that can work directly in the IDE and coach developers away from making mistakes that would be caught in later steps in the DevOps process.

When working with large-scale implementations, you should pay special attention to the several varieties of vulnerabilities that can work their way into your products. The most common pattern is using a tool like PMD to review coding best practices and identify antipatterns that allow for SQL injection and other self-inflicted problems.

It's also important to monitor for shared libraries that get incorporated into your solutions through open source or proprietary components. Those components may be based on libraries that have known or discovered vulnerabilities of their own. These can be harder to track and secure than simple coding patterns.

Designing for DevOps and Release Management (Beware of "Darkitecture")

One of the accepted best practices in Salesforce is "use the most appropriate tool for each task." This philosophy keeps you and your users on the best possible path for taking advantage of upgrades and improvements made within the platform. The wide variety of component types can make regimented deployment of functionality complicated. It's very important to have a clear idea of the types of deployments that are easy and those that can require significantly more work. I'll coin and use the word *darkitecture* to describe system or logical components designed solely to enable a certain type of phased deployment. Some of the common design patterns that require building a supporting darkitecture are A/B testing, feature toggling, dark releases, and limited roll-outs.

DevOps in Salesforce is about managing units of change across the many different components within the platform. Most of the changes you can make are manageable as pieces of metadata and can be moved from instance to instance (org to org). Once a component is initialized on the platform, it is part of the platform. Even if end users don't have permission to see it, the component exists and can be built upon by others with admin rights. Adding new features or enabling new functionality is easy. Removing things or turning things "off" brings complications because you are pushing changes to a single instance. This instance is running all of your code and configurations together, and there is no real mechanism to maintain isolation of configuration changes. There are mechanisms to hide or show most of the components you use for functionality, but they're not the same for all components. Each component type can require a different structure to prevent it from being used or seen.

For example, a Lightning app is a logical container for users that is composed of different views of different objects. Those objects might be used by many other Lightning apps. If updates to your Lightning app include changes to the underlying objects, all those other apps might be impacted. To continue this example, if you wanted to change the way some field behaves but not change it for all the places that use the field currently, you could create a new field. Your plan might be to eventually remove the older fields or make your changes to the "in use" fields. These extra fields that may or may not be redundant and are only there to facilitate a transition are an example of darkitecture. It is not ideal to have this sort of redundancy, but it is created to keep the old functions from being affected by the new functions.

Darkitecture might take the form of a temporary permission set used to let only certain users see a feature (keeping the feature *dark* to the others). It could also take the form of logical branches in Apex code that refer to code running only when certain conditions are met. For example, you might create a "Custom Setting" or "Custom Label" flag called NEW_FEATURE_ENABLED. This flag would be set to false until you were ready to have your new feature take effect. Once you were ready for it to be true all the time—when you were no longer A/B testing or previewing the feature—you would no longer need this flag. But if you went on to build other components that relied on this new feature and needed to be tested, what would happen if it were set to false again? Taking the feature offline would also impact other features that had not been built to tolerate that feature going offline.

Darkitecture injects hard-to-discover dependencies and points of failure into your functionality. It's also a form of technical debt that should be cleaned up when it no longer serves a purpose. Here, I gave individual examples of keeping a single atomic component dark. Modern features are made up of many components. Keeping track of all the temporary constructs that you would need to create to toggle (or A/B test) a complex feature set is laborious. Failing to appropriately manage all of the potential crossovers of one toggled component with other toggled components could be disastrous.

If this is something you are going to attempt, design your DevOps pipeline and sandbox structure accordingly. In most cases, it's best to deal with darkitecture structures in your development process rather than in your production code/configuration. It's cleaner to create multiple test environments to conditionally combine and test your new functions than to build in a bunch of interdependent conditional logic in your production code. If your organization is at the maturity level to desire this level of development complexity, it probably already has enough complexity to track and manage in its traditional functions. Extra complexity exacts a heavy toll when onboarding new builders/developers and adds points of failure. Ultimately, this slows future development and can create a fragile environment.

Properly planned, darkitecture can be done with technical debt and risk minimized. The logical scaffolding to support a complex deployment practice can be created and documented for easy application, though this will mean foregoing some of the intuitive best practices for simpler organizations. Polymorphism may have to give way to discrete and moderate redundant structures. Good naming schemes and separation of intents will be critical. Data storage and code size will also be impacted. Some of these changes may have performance or licensing implications to consider as well.

One of the few good reasons to adopt a multi-org structure (where your company uses multiple production instances of Salesforce) is to provide isolation between different types of development methodologies. A high-stakes customer org with customer-facing or revenue-generating functions should not be the same org that employees are encouraged to be creative within (a citizen development org). Rapid development and loose standards are ideal in some cases, but not in others. This should be evaluated before launching a Salesforce implementation. Good architects will raise a flag any time the fundamental usage model of Salesforce (including these backend considerations) changes. Make your designs as simple as they should be, but no simpler.

The Good

The variety of automation and code promotion systems available to Salesforce developers has increased in recent years. The internal offerings, with DevOps Center on top of Changesets, are strong enough for most medium to large teams. Larger teams will probably benefit from third-party tools, but they're not required. The integration plug-ins that work with VS Code are also improving to enable easy code promotion and automation functions, and VS Code supports code coaching functions to help teams align on standards and best practices.

If you are bringing in consulting firms or other experienced practitioners, you will likely get pushed to invest in many of the toolsets described in this chapter. The compliance requirements, size, and sensitivity of your company/industry will dictate whether these tools are necessary for your development pipeline.

The Gotchas

Salesforce's DevOps ecosystem is not as easily automated as some other systems and platforms. There are still a handful of manual steps required, and some quirks to learn about. Furthermore, DevOps is a hefty skill to have to add to a developer's toolset. Each new set of DevOps tools and practices requires at least some learning and onboarding. It may also require a specialized team of experts. Make sure you have the long-term appetite for the investment as you size your pipelines and teams. The extra training required on the processes to build your features is not insignificant. If you already have a healthy DevOps pipeline, you may end up duplicating some key resources to work with Salesforce. Do a full proof of concept of a pipeline before building your estimates. SSO and integration "gotchas" can pop up where you least expect them. This is especially true in hybrid or on-premises infrastructures. Cloud-hosted platforms tend to favor integrating with other cloud-hosted platforms.

The other drawback of the large numbers of ways that exist to create solutions is just that: there are often a lot of ways to do the same thing. Each person may see a solution as a different set of parts. This can lead to a bit of a melange of approaches, and the worst part is trying to reverse engineer how something works after the builder is gone. Large implementations need to dedicate time and resources to mapping how functionality is built. Systems that function extremely well can be labyrinthine landfills without a clear map from a well-executed plan. Currently, no Salesforce DevOps tools provide this framework or enable this discipline. Compliance and architecture have to have a hand in the checks and balances as well.

The Growth

At the time of writing, DevOps maturity is an exciting domain to watch in Salesforce. The in-platform DevOps Center and Salesforce-specific tools like Copado, AutoRABIT, and Elements.cloud show signs of catapulting Salesforce past its competition. Self-documenting frameworks and story-to-element mapping could greatly reduce the technical debt common to rapid delivery systems such as Salesforce. Organizations that need DevOps tools beyond those included with the platform should invest in multiple suites to track functionality, security, and other facets of architecture. Acquisitions and integrations make this even more vitally important.

Summary

Salesforce has made most of the development functionality of the platform available to third parties. This means that a lot of the rapid innovation will come from outside the native Salesforce ecosystem. Watch closely for continued developments in this space so that you can take advantage of these new tools. Keep your eyes on the AppExchange and third-party offerings, free and paid. Scale your investment in architects and architects' tools as you add development resources. Investing in the right tools at the right time (data factories, web service mock frameworks, data migration and scrubbing tools) can help keep your costs down and your time to market fast. Don't just scale your process; make sure you evolve it.

The other side of the coin with the wide usage of these tools is that they are almost a requirement for experienced developers. Not having a Git repo or other similar tools can disorient developers who are accustomed to these modern trappings. If you have an organization large enough to warrant an enterprise architecture practice, you will probably need to be well versed in DevOps. Salesforce DevOps may require an investment in one or several additional tools of the types described in this chapter. With DevOps, as with security, you should always have a little more than you need, but not more. Don't purchase tools or add processes that don't justify their value; you should always be able to financially justify any process or purchase.

CHAPTER 11

The Architect

In the previous chapters we have covered many of the foundational Salesforce technology concepts. Now we will dive into more of the specifics of the role of an architect working with Salesforce. As we touched on in Chapter 5, *architect* definitely makes the list of commonly misused and confused terms in the world of information technology, and it has no clearer a definition in Salesforce than in any other realm. The distinctions between the different definitions are blurry at best, and just about every one is met with exceptions and objections.

To start the conversation, we will use a very simple definition, and we'll expand from there. As you'll see in this chapter, there are many different roles an architect can take in a project, and they can be spread across many different job titles. Some of the most skilled architects I have worked with blended project management, business analysis, user experience, and client relationship skills to deliver complex masterpieces of functionality. I have also met many architects who have gathered diverse hands-on building or development skills throughout their careers. Whether these roles are specified in a job title or distributed across one or several people depends on the scale of the effort. Most of the time, anyone with a perspective of these roles' goals will decide how much time to spend focusing on each. Many of these concepts only become critical in larger projects, or when you have many teams to coordinate. As you are planning your project, you will want to apply communication processes and add documentation and diagramming to your plans.

Builders Versus Architects

A *builder* creates things with a defined set of skills or tools. Developers, engineers, and designers are some examples of builders. Builders usually work in a specific horizontal or vertical realm. A *full stack engineer* builds at multiple tiers in the same vertical or horizontal. ("Full stack" can also mean that this person writes both frontend and backend code: data access and data display.)

An *architect* builds plans to assemble various components across multiple stacks into a compound solution. The architect's skill is multidimensional, requiring enough knowledge of the traits of each of those components to recommend an effective, holistic solution. The solution must take into account not only the technical aspects but also other facets of the entire scenario, such as budget, security, system resources, employee resources, skill sets, long-term maintenance, performance, processes, success measures, exposures, communication, fit, and stakeholder alignment.

The roles of builder and architect are not mutually exclusive. The growth of the Salesforce ecosystem has created many builder-architects. Maybe the funnier definition is true: "Those who can't build, architect." My favorite analogy as a project architect is taking on the role of a certain web-slinging superhero. Seeing things that need to be connected and locking them together by creating a bridge of understanding. Sharing the relationships between indirectly connected concepts. Shooting webs of understanding to connect people and ideas. Just your friendly neighborhood pattern-human.

The Different Types of Architect Roles

The variety of roles that an architect can play in large Salesforce implementation or customization projects is vastly unappreciated. It's also difficult to assign a direct value to the role of the architect in keeping a project aligned to a bigger picture. As with security roles, their value often only becomes apparent after something goes wrong due to their absence. Some roles are forward-looking, operating in a green field with fewer operational requirements. However, many, if not most, are essentially support roles. To be clear, though these are all roles that are widely recognized and commonly encountered in a Salesforce context, it is unlikely that these will be official titles on a project team. Architects often fill several of these roles rather than focusing on a single area.

Success Architect

The role of a Success Architect is a bit hard to define, but it can deliver very concrete value in large projects. Everyone working on a project is responsible for its success. The Success Architect looks at the plan for the project and tries to foresee and resolve any problems that the plan might create or encounter.

Success Architects often solve problems with people processes more than technical solutions. One of my favorite contributions as a Success Architect was to predict the growth and attrition of team members over a large, multiyear project. We required each team to create a storybook of functionality, combined with highly visual system maps. This is a good practice that can regularly fall by the wayside because of budget constraints and other priorities, but due to the specific pace of this project, the help it provided in enabling fast onboarding of new members proved critical to success.

Success Architects will need to adapt to issues faced in real time as well as predicting bottlenecks or challenges and working to mitigate them. Another niche example of a process born of the observation of a keen Success Architect was the alignment of release cadences that varied drastically. Delivery of an integration project required four systems to consecutively provide data to a final system. All four systems had different release timings and windows. If we hadn't planned and coordinated the required changes to each downstream system at the beginning of the project, this could have resulted in a massive bottleneck and caused delays. Spotting this iceberg early in the project and coordinating all of the team's disparate releases was a novel challenge with a critical outcome.

Foresight, adaptability, and communication are the key traits of the Success Architect, who often works on the high-visibility challenges of a project. Figure 11-1 outlines the core focus of this role.

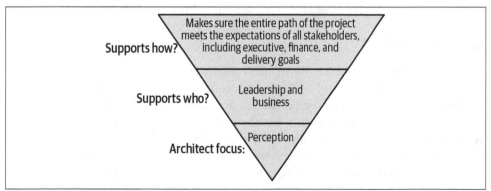

Figure 11-1. The role and focus of the Success Architect

Operational (Project) Architect

The Operational Architect is the more day-to-day, in-the-present version of the Success Architect. They keep the project on the technical path and navigate all the technical challenges, keeping teams operating at peak efficiency. They're the escalation point for all technical teams within their scope, and they serve as the tie-breaker and champion for key decisions faced by any of those teams. The Operational Architect makes sure that the solution described as "the plan" is adhered to and that the desired outcomes are achieved. This key player is at the intersection of DevOps, development, user experience, project management, and security. They may also be referred to as a tech lead or technical architect.

This is more of a tactical role, so the Operational Architect doesn't get to prioritize documentation or strategy. Key traits are an ability to listen and keep a balance between priorities. The Operational Architect will also maintain communication with other teams. They know when and how to escalate critical issues.

Figure 11-2 outlines the core focus of the Operational Architect.

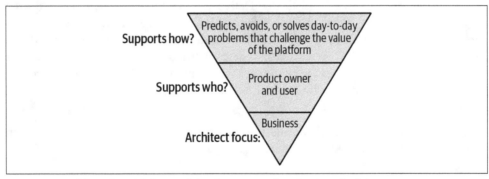

Figure 11-2. The role and focus of the Operational or Project Architect

Solution Architect

The Solution Architect creates the detailed technical plan for addressing the business requirements of a project and decides which components and features to use to build a solution. They may also be responsible for designing the data model used for a solution. These are extremely valuable members of any Salesforce team. They are often very experienced builders and know the most effective way to deliver functionality within Salesforce. I have seen every tenure of technician in this role, from senior developer or admin to senior enterprise architect. On every project team, there's someone in the role of Solution Architect (or at least who is responsible for delivering solution architecture). Usually a Solution Architect is delivering solutions in a single stack—specifically Salesforce—so this role does not really meet our previous definition of an architect (it might more accurately be called *Solution Engineer*).

Figure 11-3 outlines the core focus of the Solution Architect. This role maps fairly directly to the Application Architect certification pathway within the Salesforce certification ecosystem.

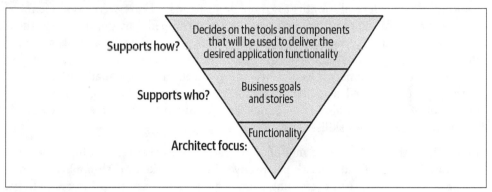

Figure 11-3. *The role and focus of the Solution Architect*

UX Architect

The UX Architect is another unsung hero in the trenches of a project that can have a huge impact on its success. They keep a constant eye on all of the technical goals that affect the final reception of the product by the consumer.

While executing a project, tiny changes in scope or approach can have a large cumulative effect on the final result. Everything from the performance of integrations to the net perceived value of the end product has to be tracked and accounted for. This is especially true in Agile projects, where the delivery expectations are expected to change.

> *User experience* is sometimes interpreted to mean *user interface*, but there's more to it than that. Put simply, the user experience is the sum of all of the user interactions with an application or brand. The user experience can be bad due to many factors not necessarily in the control of the application. A set of pages can have the perfect font, good contrast, and very clear wording, but the user experience can still be terrible if they're not adapted to the situation at hand. If you are developing in multiple channels (telephone, chat, web or mobile) and the user has access to all of them, the cumulative effects of all the interfaces come into play. The UX Architect manages the full scope of interaction, including performance and outside influences along with in-page impact.

Wearing this hat, I once managed to put myself out of a job. Of a large set of features planned for a customer-facing application, a small percentage were dropped from the scope during the first weeks of the project. The remaining feature list was long, and it would have taken several months to complete just those. There were good technical reasons for removing all of the features that were dropped, but unfortunately those were the ones that represented most of the draw for the customer to actually go to the site. Everything that was retained was important to the business, but there was no motivation for a customer to *want* to use the application. After I made this observation and communicated it to the client, the project was quickly shut down, saving them a lot of money but also putting my team out of work. Fortunately, they quickly found other uses for our skills!

Applications that make use of multiple integrations can also face timing issues that should be reviewed from a user's perspective. I once worked on an application that had been designed to read everything from a single "source of truth" in order to get the most accurate values. Later functions were designed to send updates (write) to a "source of record" to reduce load on the source of truth. This might not seem like a bad design decision, until you consider the case where two consecutive calls write data and expect to read it immediately after. This caused a problem, because the downstream synchronization between the source of record and the source of truth was a nightly process. This meant that there could be as much as a 24-hour lag between new data being written and that data being available for reads. Imagine getting a message like, "You have successfully updated your credit card information. Please return to the site tomorrow to make a purchase." Clearly, this issue had to be rectified before the site went live to avoid a tragic user experience.

Figure 11-4 outlines the core focus of the UX Architect, who is responsible for making sure that all the components involved contribute to the best possible user experience.

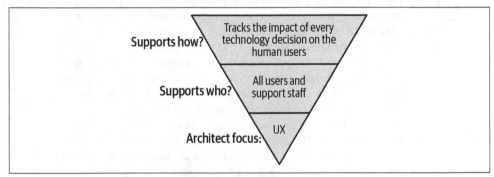

Figure 11-4. The role and focus of the UX Architect

The Certified Technical Architect (CTA)

Salesforce has an excellent certification track for Technical Architects. The certification pathway involves passing about 10 exams, culminating in one or more panel interviews. During these interviews, you are given a written scenario describing a business's need for Salesforce functionality. Your task is to plan and diagram a solution that meets all of the business's criteria with the functionality of the core platform. You can include other adjacent products if they make sense to fill the requirements, but these should mostly be covered by Sales Cloud and Service Cloud functionality. You get three hours to review the scenario and prepare your solution model and diagrams. After a short break, you have 45 minutes to present your solution to the panel of experts, followed by another 40 minutes of Q&A to defend it. The panel digs into your solution across several domains: security, data, integration, etc. It is not uncommon for candidates to take multiple years to prepare for this exam, and they are vetted at an extreme level. The goal is to ensure that CTAs can quickly and thoroughly conceive and describe solutions to meet any needs within the Salesforce platform.

The body of knowledge required to succeed in this panel exam is focused around Salesforce: development in Salesforce, security in Salesforce, data modeling in Salesforce, integrations in Salesforce, authentication in Salesforce. So, while the CTA exam is the most big-picture architecture exam that Salesforce has, it is mostly limited to this single platform. If you think of an architect as someone who constructs solutions with multiple platforms, you might consider this more of an application-building exam. That being said, every Salesforce CTA I have worked with has had extensive knowledge of other systems and architecture patterns. I don't believe you can get to this level of Salesforce fluency without an underlying knowledge of the deep structures that multiplatform architects are familiar with.

Figure 11-5 shows an overview of the timeline and structure of the CTA certification pathway.

Studying for and passing the CTA exam is a very hot topic of discussion among Salesforce architects. You can almost guarantee that CTAs will be very good at all of the architect roles described in this chapter. Other certifications can be acquired without the requisite experience required to actually perform in those roles; the CTA exam is the exception.

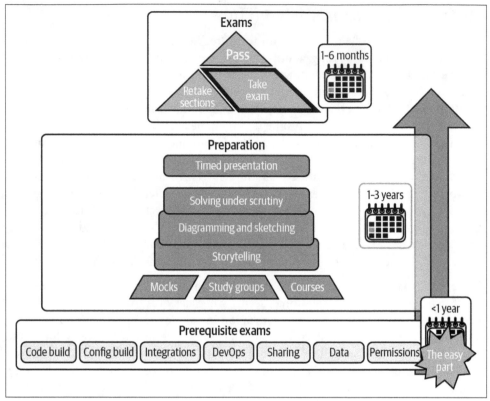

Figure 11-5. The CTA certification pathway

Communication

One of the main ways that an architect can keep a project aligned is through structured communications. Like it or not, this involves having meetings. A good way to keep meetings productive is to have a good set of central documents to regularly review and sign off on. Work with project leadership to make this process mandatory and part of the formal project ceremonies. Work sessions to collaborate on these artifacts are usually necessary.

Establishing a regular cadence of Architecture Review Board (ARB) meetings can help in maintaining clear lines of communication and project artifacts. Encourage regular cameo appearances by leadership to keep them prioritized. You should also invite architects and engineers with advanced perspectives. If you have access to a security or data architecture team, they make good partners as well.

A primary focus of ARB meetings should be around making and/or documenting and communicating *decisions*, aligned around long-term and short-term success metrics. Establishing the appropriate level of detail for these decisions is more of an art than a science. Decisions can be made by the ARB, made independently by teams, or made by teams and escalated to the ARB for review. Logging and sharing decisions that don't require escalation is a great way of creating breadcrumbs to illustrate the path and trajectory of a project. This becomes crucial when you are dealing with a large number of teams.

Decisions generally qualify for bringing to an ARB for review if they:

- Generate a drastic change in the technical approach from what was originally planned. Examples include:
  — New integration
  — Alteration in permission structure
  — Purchase of a third-party component
  — Creation of a reusable component
- Cause a change to the direct costs of the project or ensuing maintenance costs.
- Create technical debt that will or might exact a toll later.
- Describe a significant milestone for the progress of the project.
- Provide insurance against 20/20 hindsight challenges and absentee stakeholders.
- Will not be boring to leadership.

A well-maintained decision log can provide a vital record of the technical components of the project. A normal team should generate one to five loggable decisions per sprint.

Documentation

Another communication asset for architecture practitioners is documentation. It can be very difficult to give documentation duties priority over other immediate concerns, but this should be seen as the primary success measure for an architect. The key to a successful architecture documentation practice is having a well-thought-out plan backed by a process that requires regular updates and communication of critical changes. The ARB meetings and decision documentation described in the previous section should be wired into your documentation practice. Schedule review sessions (alone or with stakeholders) to create a cadence for updating documents. Make appointments for yourself to ensure you get it done.

Make sure to date stamp your documents. Always assume that the document you are working on now is the only and best document that someone will find. Provide as much context about "now" as you can. This will help the reader start piecing together what has happened "since." Describe the events that led to the changes from the previous state described in the previous document.

Selecting What to Document or Diagram

This is the more-art-than-science part of the architect's role. Due to the effort involved in keeping documents up to date, deciding what to spend your time and energy on is key. As mentioned previously, it is paramount to make adherence to and participation in documentation practices a mandatory part of a process. Work with leadership and project managers to outline your expectations for official project artifacts. Establish a cadence and a grading system for participation. The following sections define some of the typical tiers of diagrams and the perspectives that drive you to map them.

The city view

There are a few standard schools of thought regarding how to approach documentation. I tend to use the 4+1 architecture view model, described further in "Diagramming Practices" on page 130, as the core of any project documentation effort. I start at a very high level and create what I call a "city view" of a project, looking at it from a few perspectives. This top-level, all-encompassing view is critical because it can serve as a visual "table of contents" for all of your other documentation. Make sure to take the appropriate amount of time to keep your top-level view up to date. The path that the architect forges is useless if no one can follow along with your designs.

Complexity

You should adapt your diagrams and documentation to respond as soon as complexity or confusion pops up. We've already discussed how some of the seemingly simplest terms, like *application*, can have many meanings. Not clarifying the definitions early on can cause critical stakeholder alignment problems. You can't expect your colleagues to just "go to Trailhead" and catch up on all of your accumulated understanding.

The inspiration for this book was the large number of lasting friendships I have made based on being able to work across communication and paradigm barriers to explain Salesforce. Share your vision regularly. If you see confusion, address it. Bear in mind that complexity can have many different definitions. Do your best to anticipate the components that will be used by multiple teams, and make sure they're all on the same page. Factor in long-term skill set planning for teams that will take over support after the implementation is done. Product owners and architects who own the infrastructure in the long term will want to understand when new features are added—especially those features that will add to the list of skills required to support the solution.

Points of failure

Clearly marking pieces of an architecture that are prone to failure or might have little or no signaling of failure is key for the long-term support of a project. Integrations with different technologies are obvious candidates when building a map of support concerns. Data maintained by end users is another possible point of failure. These failure points are also an area of interest for security teams, who will primarily be concerned with the interfaces between systems that have different types of usage vulnerabilities. For this audience, focus on details that will help them understand the technical skeleton without having to filter out all of the functional concepts.

Figure 11-6 shows a simple diagram that maps the points of failure in a project, mixing both functional and technical concepts. Such a diagram may not be a long-term core document, but it's good to communicate this information up front, for stakeholder buy-in and support. This is also a very good candidate for decision tracking (discussed earlier).

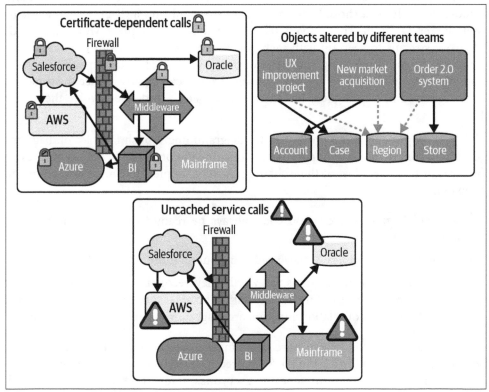

Figure 11-6. Sample mapping of points of failure

The UX Architect has a strong presence here. Often neglected during design, the administrators and support teams for all applications are also critical personas to design around. Decisions that create less likely or impactful points of failure can get ignored. One of the more tangible arguments for following best practices can be to expose these as technical debt or increases to potential support costs in the long term.

It's also important to identify a stakeholder who has experience dealing with each of the points of failure—someone who has been responsible for repairing issues caused by creating or running afoul of gaps in strategy and planning. Incorporating their feedback and critiques during a project can provide valuable support for nonfunctional solution design patterns and goals.

Diagramming Practices

Everything in this book should fit into some mental model or paradigm for the aspiring enterprise architect. If the distinction between two terms or concepts (or more importantly, why you should care) isn't clear, stop and find a diagram that explains them better. Diagrams are also very useful for helping an architect who spans multiple work streams to keep up with each. Reading bodies of stories in Jira or meeting notes can be mind-numbing and waste of time. Outlining in diagrams the concepts you expect to be monitored and kept informed about can greatly reduce the time and effort required to stay aligned. Use these diagrams as a start, then evolve them over time.

This section presents some starter tips for diagramming. I push for a lot of diagrams to be delivered by projects as part of their documentation, as large bodies of text can be difficult to parse. Most of these should stay very simple. Here are a few axioms to keep in mind:

- A good diagram is like good code: always be ready to refactor if it becomes too complex.
- Make things as complex as they need to be, but no more.
- People tend to scan diagrams for words they recognize, which puts a lens of expectation on the rest of the relationships. It can be very helpful to walk viewers through the types of relationships you are diagramming and who they are for.

There are a lot of good architecture diagramming practices listed in the Diagrams section (*https://oreil.ly/ApT2z*) of the Salesforce Architects website. The biggest struggle is trying to make diagrams appeal to everyone's unique perspective. I try to stick to two types of diagrams: *logical/conceptual* and *physical/system*. In projects, I like to own (and control updates to) the highest-level diagrams and let others use those as templates/references to draw more granular versions or variations. Attempting to maintain strict consistency is generally a fool's errand.

Publishing documents early and often to maintain group awareness is the best possible approach to fighting "perspective chaos." Make them easy to find and include in PowerPoint presentations, and they may go viral. This is *very* important when working on large projects or in large organizations. Diagrams can be for you, but they should also be for sharing. Keep other people in mind when you build them. Also, don't try to put too much into a single view. Some tools, like Lucid and Miro, allow for easy zooming in and out. I have had mixed results trying to use tools like these to put more content into a single canvas; again, keeping it simple is usually best.

The 4+1 architectural view model (*https://oreil.ly/KCTLm*) is a great starting place for building good diagramming practices. This model focuses on using multiple perspectives of projects and systems to make sure all facets are represented. When dealing with hybrid infrastructures that include both cloud and on-premise resources, considering different perspectives is an absolute must. Most of the project killers are found when crossing system or security boundaries. The primary facets of the 4+1 view model are the following perspectives (the "+1" refers to example use cases or scenarios that illustrate the design, providing a fifth view):

- Physical (systems and network)
- Logical (functionality, concepts, and data flow)
- Development (memory, environments, sandboxes, and apps)
- Process (data, timings, batches, connections)

These are a great foundation, but depending on the project, adding more (or more specific versions of these) may help your colleagues gain perspective.

My version of the +1 substitutes user experience flow for technical usage scenarios. It's very important to fully map what leads a user to using your application. You can then build everything that's required to serve that need. This should be bookended by all of the user's expected outcomes. This process is akin to journey mapping, and having this perspective can save many hours of work on extra features that seem like they might be beneficial but end up being confusing or frustrating. We've all called a business phone number and been asked at the outset, "Would you be willing to stay on the line and participate in a survey after this call?" Seems reasonable, right? But would that be okay for a 911 or other emergency call too? What if help never arrived? These are solution design flaws, not application design flaws, and should be handled by a UX Architect. Ideally the UX and journey mapping exercise would be done prior to system mapping, but in Agile project processes, directions can change. Without a reference architecture for user motivations and expectations, applications can miss delivering a usable tool.

If working with more than one platform, you should also add a "Data and Encryption" perspective. I usually merge this with either the Logical view or the Physical view. Make sure to document all of the helper systems that assist in the transitioning of data across boundaries. Examples include ETL scripts, caching layers, file exports, and middleware. Maintaining a full perspective of these pieces can keep systems that might otherwise be forgotten in view.

My most successful diagramming strategy involves mapping a project based on what is common and what is unique to the key concepts that are valid for that project. You'll need to make multiple diagrams. Diagrams should be used to illustrate *a few* concepts, not everything. For each one, the technical focus of the audience should be clear.

Having a map of your diagrams and what they illustrate is a must for good architectural practice. If you're following these standards, going forward, every diagram should indicate three things clearly:

1. Why/when?
2. What are the key concepts/groups?
3. What are the important details?

You'll need to scale the parts of the diagram to cover whatever types of complexity you are dealing with. Figure 11-7 shows an example of a simple high-level techno-functional diagram. Something like this may be fine if you are dealing with a complete greenfield system and no other teams, with no integrations or other variables to account for. For projects that include any kind of growth or scale, you should attempt to map and keep track of where your functionality starts to expand.

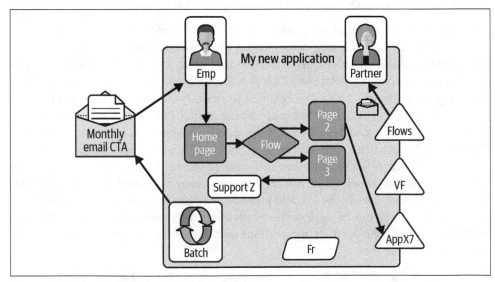

Figure 11-7. A simple techno-functional diagram

Where Should I Start?

Diagramming strategy becomes a requirement when you need to manage an effort at different levels of detail or across multiple concepts (e.g., functionality diagrams or networking diagrams). It can help to make the simplest diagram that references elements of all the important concepts you are managing first. This high-level document is your navigation level, or table of contents. It frames or creates a map of your other concepts/diagrams to make sure people know what is being attempted. Try not to have overlapping concepts at this level; it's mostly about setting expectations for the next level. (Consider how different "a map of the world" would look to personas like a traveler, a ship's captain, or a marine biologist.)

Insufficient context can cause people to reject your organizational structure and either miss the point or, worse, draw their own diagrams. Having a broad title or vague context can lead to contributors not knowing what details belong in the diagram and what needs to be documented in some other fashion. They should work together to make this clear. When it comes to the details, less is more. The tendency can be to include too much; if the details in a diagram are obscuring its intended focus, rebuild it. Be ready to move extraneous details to another diagram or document.

The practice of analyzing projects and infrastructures in terms of "shearing layers," or layers of change, has been around for many years. It started as a physical building architecture approach and has been adopted by many in the IT industry. Gartner calls this the *Pace-Layered Application Strategy* (*https://oreil.ly/esB8f*). The concept (roughly) is to divide a project or application into domains based on variations in either adaptability or dependability. This is very simple to say, but learning how to apply it will come with experience. Pick two or three of the following list of perspectives to create your top layers. Apply the same types of rationalizations as you go down into layers with more detail:

- Standard object use
- Storage requirements
- Data compliance concerns
- Data sensitivity
- Data exposure
- Encryption standards
- Business data concepts

- Customer versus employee interactions
- Regular versus occasional access
- Network, internet, or physical location
- Functional capabilities
- Key processes
- Derived value or revenue
- Supported languages
- Accessibility

Clearly label the diagrams so that newcomers will know exactly what data they will find there and what they won't. This will be even more critical when you share responsibility for the diagrams with others. A large amount of the push that people have for diagramming is to show that they have done something. They will try to place their updates in the first location they find. A "diagram by committee" approach can ruin your structure. Keep community diagramming locations limited in number and scope. They should also be constantly reviewed.

Figure 11-8 is a sample of an application map with some curated components. On the left is a curated list of in-scope applications that may be integrated with directly or need to be associated due to functional overlap. At the top are the concerned users for each application. When working on large projects, having a referenceable and reusable list of personas for security and testing is critical. On the right and at the bottom are other sample aspects that may or may not have relevance to your program. Shared objects, code frameworks, business processes, mobile devices, third-party licenses, and geographic locations are other examples that might be critical perspectives to give about your project.

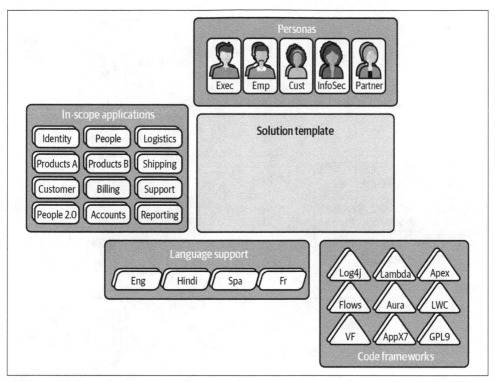

Figure 11-8. Sample project topology template

Figure 11-9 shows how an application engineer could use this template as a starting point to diagram how their application fits into a project. Having an understanding of the high-level process flows and concepts of an application can help newcomers quickly orient to the overall project landscape.

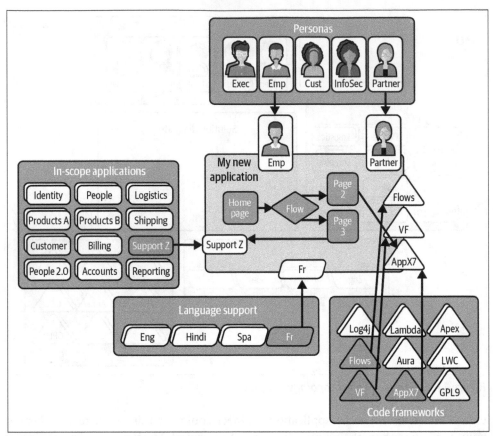

Figure 11-9. An example of a filled-out project topology diagram with a single application

Figure 11-10 illustrates how you can expand this model to hold more applications. The value of this shared concept map is realized when different teams can see areas of overlap or collaborate to create shared resources. Regular rally meetings to confirm whether Team X is still purely focused on Process A can spark discussions about overlap and keep teams coloring within their lines. This view can also humanize status calls and burndown reports by showing the relationships between people and processes.

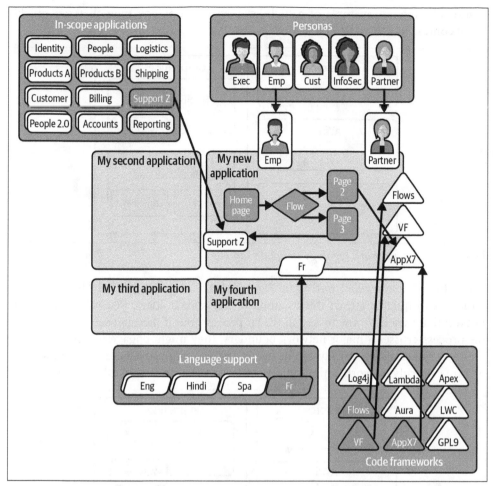

Figure 11-10. High-level application map with room for multiple applications

Creating reusable templates can also make your life easier. Your high-level diagrams should be required header slides for all technical presentations. When working on larger implementations, I require two slides in each ARB submission taken from the top-level diagram master: techno-functional capability relevance and a network security topology map. Those two slides bring the business and security stakeholders to awareness quickly. You want the right audience in the loop for important decisions, regardless of any confusing acronyms or jargon. You also want to reduce the risk of and culpability for not properly informing the relevant groups. You have to build awareness before you can garner consensus.

Figure 11-11 is an example of a high-level system topology map that can quickly bring context to a discussion.

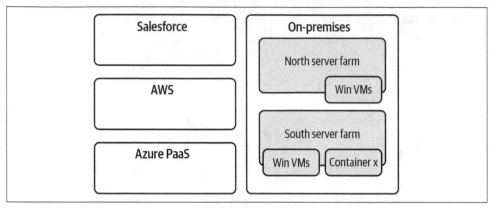

Figure 11-11. A network topology template sample

With this template filled out as in Figure 11-12, a meeting titled "Problem with Orders" can quickly attract the attention of key stakeholders. Firewall teams might not feel that they have any role in the order process, but if they can see at a glance that the process crosses a major network boundary, they might engage to help. Engaging the right stakeholders quickly can be key in fast-moving projects or environments. A picture can truly be worth a thousand words, and even more valuable minutes.

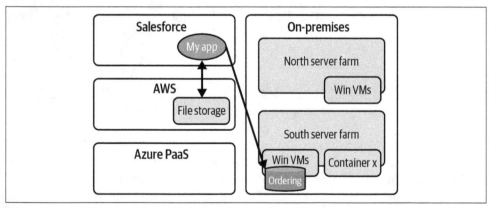

Figure 11-12. The network topology template with application components

After you have established what key concepts you are going to track throughout the project, it's a great idea to follow a layered approach, adding more detail as you go. There's some good detail on the "levels" paradigm on the Salesforce Architects website (*https://oreil.ly/6xmXX*), but the following are some of my primary guidelines. Good, well-communicated documentation with a well-adopted diagramming plan will pay for itself over time.

What Are the Key Concepts/Groups? (Level 0)

At this level it's okay to show relationships and overlap. Actually, that's most of what you should be doing at "Level 0." Start with your title and audience. Then make your main concepts big and label them clearly. Explain the scope of the diagram if you didn't make it clear in the navigation diagrams.

Here are some examples of clear diagram titles and scopes:

- Master data by network location for disaster recovery
- Functional responsibilities by development group
- DLP exposure map by data type
- Functional design by user experience interface
- Products and prices by contract term types

A good pattern to follow is "*this* by *that* for *them*." Don't try to create too many dimensions or include too many details. Level 0 diagrams should be concept maps and point to deeper-dive diagrams that are domain-specific.

You may end up with multiple views of the big picture, and that's okay. Try to keep it narrowed down to just a few, or make sure that the relationships are clear via content and naming.

What Are the Important Details? (Level 1)

Level 1 diagrams can be created by enterprise architects as frameworks or expectations but should be maintained by domain architects or SMEs. They can include links to data or other repositories. The responsibility for maintaining diagrams that deal with details at lower levels can be shared with other participating leadership teams, but they should be regularly reviewed and updated by a primary owner. Accountability is key. These leaders should care whether their segments of responsibility are well represented publicly. Praise and comparisons at regularly scheduled intervals are your tools to incentivize keeping these diagrams up to date.

The Details (Levels 2+)

Responsibility for building out and maintaining documentation at level 2 and beyond should be delegated to others. These documents can be diagrams, spreadsheets, or text. Not everything lends itself to shapes and colors. Scale the number of levels according to your project's complexity, and periodically review it. People tend to find a location and make it their home for everything. Curating what is "inside" and what is "outside" of your documentation and diagramming domain can be the most difficult aspect of maintaining a documented view of a project, visual or otherwise.

Don't try to maintain too many diagrams or go too many levels deep. It's better to have a few high-quality, well-maintained diagrams than many that won't be kept up or found.

Where Does It Stop?

Most of what I've discussed here is just good information architecture practice and is not specific to enterprise or Salesforce architecture. The principles are shared. If you have been in an architectural role for a long time, none of this will be new to you. If you are new in an architect role, it will be up to you to decide how wide or deep you go, but the large majority of Salesforce projects don't need any more than two or three layers of documentation. The most important thing is to clearly communicate a plan and make sure you have the time to maintain it.

Acting Like an Architect

Depending on the size of your project team, an architect may have to be a people manager and not just a technology manager. The greater your breadth of oversight, the more people you will need to align and interconnect. An architect may be viewed as a superhero, connecting teams with unifying concepts. Alternatively, an architect may be seen as a supervillain, demanding heavy rework and adding lots of academic nonfunctional requirements that stall delivery. If people don't understand the peril you are saving them from, you will likely be seen as a burden.

Just as a refresher, we are defining an architect as a person who's responsible for assembling diverse components into a compound solution (this is my big-picture definition, among a very blurry world of titles and roles). The components are considered at the application level, not at the level of lines of code or buttons with actions, and an architect might have many Solution Architects reporting to them that they must coordinate and orchestrate.

The most important first step is to establish a list of priorities. These will be social and technical responsibilities, and they will vary greatly from project to project based on scope and available resources. Some priorities you may need to consider are:

- Making time for questions
- Fighting fires and emergencies
- Root cause analysis/postmortem communications
- Documentation
- Leadership connections (managing up)
- Inspection and reviews:

- Security
- Code standards
- Nonfunctional requirements
- Running ARB meetings
- Amending processes
- Team building
- Learning and education
- Teaching
- Starting fires (breaking things) to test processes

Many architects fall into the trap of being either too hands-on or not enough. Losing perspective or missing the big picture is a common trap for architects. Keeping the right balance and communicating your priorities to leadership is key. Documenting the value of a full-time architect can be difficult. Make sure you are supporting valuable processes, or you won't be seen as valuable.

Identifying risks is another key value proposition for architects. This can be your primary pathway for getting tasks prioritized that are not on the functional roadmap. A risk register should be maintained by your project, or yourself if necessary. Getting risks acknowledged by leadership is the best way to keep from catching the blame when something that was preventable happens. Things do go wrong. Organizations can accept bad luck that they knew the possibility of. Surprises are seldom tolerated.

Finally, team building and "consensus farming" should be a high priority. If the project or platform is to follow your vision, your vision must be clear and well appreciated by everyone. There are no small players on a team. Everyone's voice should be important to you. If just one person doesn't know how or why to do something, your plan can fall apart. The architect is not just a technical problem solver; they're conducting an orchestra. This requires being closely connected to the vision of end users and management alike. Stay in touch with all of the guiding stars of the project so that you can adjust your plans and your teams as needed.

Along with being part of a team, you need to be okay with losing a lot of battles. The biggest difference between a senior engineer and an architect is that the engineer makes the best decision for themselves or their system, while the architect has to make the best decision for *all* systems. You may have to step in as a tie-breaker when teams are competing for resources or pitching their ideal solution. You will never build something on time or on budget where everyone gets to create their ideal solution. Someone will have to be rushed or resort to a band-aid solution. This will include you having to accept imperfect implementations of your vision from time to time. Be flexible. Live for the marathon, not the sprints.

Summary

Architects make solutions that work. Great architects make solutions that work well for everyone and survive both inevitable and unpredictable circumstances. Architects can wear many hats and provide many sources of value. Being able to envision all the components of a project and set up processes to make them work together smoothly is just one part of the job. Dealing with the unexpected and any other challenges that threaten success in any way is the other part.

Smaller projects often need good architects only during the beginning stages. Larger projects usually need a good staff of architects almost to the very end. Those architects may wear different hats along the way, perhaps participating in development or gathering and refining requirements. The architects working on any project must have skills that cover all the vital areas of the project: integrations, interactions, scale, mobile, security, etc. A good architect also looks past the creation phase and plots the successful future of an application or platform. They should actively participate in training or recruiting platform managers and governance teams to ensure ongoing success after it is launched. I have seen more than a few consulting firms that make a living off of fixing or rebuilding ungoverned platform implementations.

With an architect's perspective, you can balance and convey the need for investments beyond just the immediate and obvious. A good architect finds a path through a variety of obstacles and learns how to weigh and communicate the options. Many times, you will predict a problem but not be able to convince others to invest in avoiding it. Hopefully, people will appreciate all of the issues that didn't happen due to all of your hard work preventing them. Speak softly, and figure out how to say "I told you so" just loudly enough to not have to say it the next time. You may spend most of your time predicting things that won't be appreciated and may not come to pass in time for any personal validation; you have to become okay with this. The more tragedies you learn how to prevent, the more you have to watch happen without you being allowed to prevent them. Learning to be graceful when you are ignored is the most important skill you can acquire. You have to regulate your passion. Your relationships will be your only key to preventing *any* disasters in the future. Above all, maintain relationships as your most critical resource.

CHAPTER 12

Salesforce Well-Governed

The Salesforce platform is extremely mature in many areas. It's especially competent for small to medium-sized implementations. When you're unlocking all of the power of the platform for large sets of functionality or customization, you will need to build processes to suit the situation. In this chapter we will discuss some of the governance challenges you may face with Salesforce and how to deal with them. These aren't necessarily weaknesses of the platform, just areas that you should plan for. I have covered some of these topics in the previous chapters while discussing different features. Here, we'll expand on these extra patterns you may need to follow if you plan to grow. This should also help you predict which growth frameworks you might want to adopt before doing so becomes difficult. My primary goal, as in the previous chapters, is to enable a better understanding of the Salesforce platform. Most of the solutions presented here are common sense once you fully understand all the components in play.

Most of the topics discussed here tie back to a common theme of potential technical debt. These types of debt are possible due to a combination of features or gaps in the Salesforce platform, and not all of them will be relevant to your situation. We will look at many of the challenges you may face and talk about a few of the ways to solve (or at least attenuate) them. These approaches are not one-size-fits-all, and this chapter is not intended as an instruction manual; you may need to adapt them and should only implement those that are likely to provide value. As with all things, you should right-size your investments, aiming to mitigate risks that are likely. Looking ahead and attempting to solve tomorrow's problems today can pay off big in the long term.

Returning to the original premise of Chapter 1, Salesforce is not a single SaaS application. It's a robust infrastructure capable of delivering many different types of functionality, both purchased/licensed and personally built. It's easy to build solutions with speed and scale, but anything you manage to build "fast, cheap, and good" can lead to different types of sprawl and issues that must be addressed somewhere down the line. If you intend to use Salesforce at scale and roll your own solution, you'll need governance and discipline. Put another way, we've outlined all the gears and cogs, and now we're looking at where you may need to apply oil or schedule maintenance.

For each of the following topics, we will start by discussing the problems and their roots. Hopefully, knowing how something can get out of control and end up needing governance will shed light on how the systems at play work. Many of the "concerns" described here are common to other systems and/or cloud platforms. Actually, almost all of them are inherited from the underlying technologies they are built on, with their strengths and weaknesses. Salesforce is, of course, built on many standard technologies and is only unique in its approach and how it combines them. After discussing each concern, I'll talk about some of the governance strategies you can leverage to mitigate that concern. These, too, will be common strategies used in other systems. The only mildly unique challenges with Salesforce come from the features that make traditionally difficult functionality easy for users or developers—Salesforce, like all platforms, can suffer from the overuse of its strengths.

Data Governance

The term *data* can have many connotations within the IT vocabulary. Accordingly, many types of data governance may be required to keep your organization healthy. Salesforce handles some governance duties for you with features like automatic indexing, precomputed sharing rules, and relationship limitations. However, there are many other types of data management that you will need to keep in scope as you grow.

Concern: Data Interpretation

Using and reusing the standard objects, like Account, Contact, and Case, is strongly encouraged. When the data already stored in an object like Contact is similar to a new use case that you have, it is best practice to reuse that existing structure, even if you have to adapt it slightly to your new needs. For example, the Contact object might house information about your customers, but you might have a new requirement to store information about your employees. This should be an easy fit for the Contact object. You can either create a new RecordType or just add a new value to the "Type" picklist and have the options be either "Customer" or "Employee." You might choose to use a new RecordType if you are concerned about the security being different around the two types of Contacts. Otherwise, making sure that all connected functions know that there are two types of data in the Contact object is pretty easy.

Fast-forward a few years into the future, though, when you have 10 different types of Contacts in the Contact object. Different teams working with the data in the Contact object can step on each other's toes. This can lead to confusion and data leaks from a security perspective. It's even more likely that shared data fields will cause problems when validation rules or automation routines break when changes are made. Multiply this by dozens of shared objects and even a few teams, and you have a recipe for chaos. Following best practices and keeping the data structure too simple can actually have the opposite of the intended effect; overusing objects can make learning the underlying data concepts more difficult.

Team growth and turnover is another important factor to keep in mind when it comes to managing data definitions. There is a large performance penalty if you cannot quickly explain your data schema and relationships to incoming members of your teams. Complex, poorly documented systems lead not only to confusion and slow onboarding, but also costly mistakes.

Governance Strategies: Data Interpretation

Managing and communicating the semantic meanings of data is not a very technical chore. Diagrams with definitions and boundaries can be maintained by any participant in the project lifecycle. Mature organizations will merge an existing master data management or data architecture practice with every application platform. Maintaining a record of data definitions and scope—a *business glossary*—is core to data architecture practices (or should be). You should maintain a business glossary even if you are not incorporating Salesforce data into any other systems. ERDs can also be built with layers and transparency to assist in understanding realms and relationships. Figure 12-1 illustrates one way to map relationships between objects that have multiple definitions. Each substantially unique definition of the same object gets a representation. You would want to add a definition of each of these representations to your business glossary, outlining how they are different.

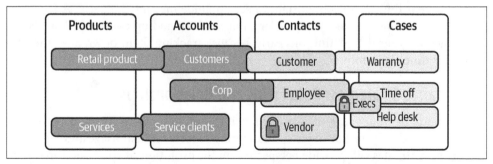

Figure 12-1. Different types of data in objects, and the relationships between them

You can also add additional dimensions to the data with a bit of work. Figure 12-2 shows additional shapes used to group together different object use concepts. If it gets too difficult to draw in two dimensions, then imagine how hard it is to learn these concepts without the drawings! Maintain a slideshow or PowerPoint deck if you have too many items to explain simply in a single diagram.

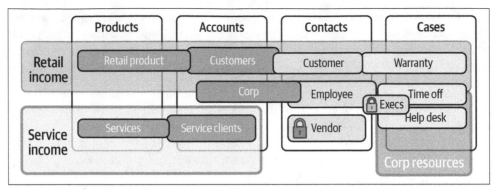

Figure 12-2. Adding additional concepts to data graphics

This may seem simple, but it's seldom done and even less often maintained. Different data structures with different definitions or behaviors within the same object are very hard to track without a proper map. In Salesforce this happens by design, so you must exercise extra discipline to manage that complexity.

Concern: Data Fields and Relationships

Another potential problem that can get away from you is having too many fields or relationships. It's a fairly common practice to create extra fields to make visualizing relationships and building reports easier. Beginning builders often create lots of fields to hold flattened hierarchical data updated by "onchange" triggers. These normalization and other wasteful practices can rapidly take you close to your limits for fields and relationships, which can stifle your plans in the future. Different objects can also have different limits, so it's important to set up guidelines for their use. A few extra fields here and there aren't a big problem, but they can add up over time. You should start tracking your data definitions early, because tracking them down after they are created is time-consuming.

Governance Strategies: Data Fields and Relationships

As you ramp up your usage of Salesforce, you should implement tracking and review processes for all of your key objects. Automating reports on field usage and highlighting the growth rates will provide perspective on the evolution of your Salesforce environment. Having a curated data dictionary with a change history will prevent many problems, but only if you review and update it frequently and share it with others. I would love to see Salesforce add the functionality of a change history for setup changes. It does provide a static "Description" field for fields, which can be used in tandem with an extract process to keep a change log, but this requires some extra effort from users. Having a tracking form as a required process for users to propose new fields and changes can be useful. This form or log can be kept in Salesforce and shared with stakeholders swiftly via reports or permissions.

Many of these mitigation strategies will require a lot of incentivization, because the benefits are seldom appreciable in the short term. Making sure to regularly highlight and reward thoughtful stewardship can provide a meaningful incentive for teammates to take the chore seriously.

Concern: Data Storage

Data storage inside of Salesforce can be costly from a licensing and productivity perspective. Salesforce is heavily tuned to be performant with many small exchanges of data. Manipulating large pieces of data, like files, is not the best use case for the platform. That said, Salesforce's attachment and file storage system has evolved over the past few years, getting more robust and performant. It now uses a binary object store structure, as opposed to BLOB storage that was more closely tied directly to object records. File storage incurs less of a resource penalty than file manipulation. As a multitenant system, memory for operations comes at a premium; more available memory means more customers per unit of hardware. Reading files into memory for alteration is hard to justify due to the very sporadic nature of the resource use required. Functionality is limited either by choice or by necessity within the platform to further the larger goal of multitenant use.

Governance Strategies: Data Storage

When looking at licensing options for a long-term storage scenario, many customers will opt to use a third-party storage provider. In my travels, Amazon S3 is the most prevalent. There are a few third-party plug-ins that convert your Salesforce org to use remote storage almost invisibly to your users, and for large organizations the cost savings are compelling. Leveraging a more file-centric system like S3 can have other benefits as well. Just remember to plan for some extra work for integrations and compliance.

Forecasting your processes' dependence on files prior to building automation or processes can save valuable time down the road. You can decide in advance how much file storage space you'll need, what integrations you'll require (like DocuSign), and what manipulations you'll need to perform (like encryption or watermarking). This kind of planning can force some conversations about retention and encryption at the same time. It's less hard work than some of the previous chores; you just need to forecast, price, compare, and optionally buy. It's quite nice when architecture challenges strongly resemble a day of shopping. Take advantage of the opportunity.

Security

Salesforce comes with a growing suite of tools to help manage security concerns. Getting a full grasp of security for an org is difficult due the variety of security structures in the platform. Some of them are easy to see and manage, while others require some digging. Good security can be defined as providing effective and reasonable protection of assets according to their value (or cost) if compromised, stolen, or destroyed. The more valuable or sensitive data is, the more steps should be taken to secure it. There are primary and secondary types of value. *Primary value* is measured solely in terms of the intrinsic value of the data. An example is the financial loss caused by fraudulent charges after a breach involving stolen credit card numbers. Another example is the work required to rebuild a piece of code that was deleted or maliciously encrypted for ransom. The *secondary value* is related to the loss of trust or faith in a brand or service offering after a breach or misuse has occurred (which can lead to lost customers/sales). Calculating the secondary value of data can be difficult, but this is an entirely necessary step in determining how to appropriately secure it.

Concern: Data Security

While Salesforce is not impenetrable, as a customer, the security of the platform is not something you need to worry about. Salesforce is constantly testing its systems against known and newly discovered vulnerabilities. As a potential customer, you can validate this yourself prior to purchase. As an architect, you should primarily be concerned with configuration blunders that might allow your data to be compromised. Configuration-based breaches and compromised accounts are the most prevalent security threats to your data in Salesforce. The threats you need to address are the people you give access to and the type of access you give them.

If you don't understand your data, you cannot secure it. It is possible to create a permission structure called "Read-Only Web Service Case Summary Profile" and allow it to have Modify All Data permissions on the entire Salesforce org. You could then grant that right to every member of the corporate softball team. It would take a very meticulous reviewer to think to check that very specifically named profile for excessive permissions. Things like this have happened, but these are not technical deficits or weaknesses in the platform; they are unbridled capabilities that require awareness, experience, and dedication to manage.

Governance Strategies: Data Security

To resolve problems with data security, you attack it from two sides. The first part of your task is keeping track of where your valuable data is located. Do regular scans for personally identifiable information (PII), personal health information (PHI), and payment card industry (PCI) data. It's strongly recommended that you use third-party tools with support for changing heuristics to keep data from evolving outside of your oversight. Salesforce has added some specific features to help you track where different types of sensitive data are stored, but these features only work if you enforce and regularly review them.

The second, equally important factor to manage is how users are getting access to data. I find it invaluable to define personas at the first imagining of any project, making sure to include all the possible candidates. Evaluating contrasting access types can help define how some users will be different from other users. Each persona must be able to claim their right to exist in the whole org security model. Defining these user domains prior to the start helps ensure that the first team doesn't build a security structure that only suits their purposes.

Profiles are the easiest security structures to understand within Salesforce, but they are intrinsically inflexible and inadequate for managing complex or multiple application structures. Nevertheless, the majority of large implementations that I see are still built upon them. The biggest hindrance with profiles is that you can only assign a user to a single profile. A given persona might need to have many access rights for some functions and fewer rights for others, but profiles don't support different personas having different roles depending on the application. Profiles also contain the license that the user is granted. Ideally, this will be the only thing that profiles are used to manage.

As use cases requiring many different types of users to be able to live in harmony and securely share Salesforce grow, the utility of profiles shrinks. Shop your profile-based security plan around to various experts, and trust the ones that say to build around permission sets and permission set groups instead. The newer permission set model allows for multiple relationships, which makes it easy for you to dream up different roles and functions and assign them to whatever combinations of users and groups you need. Seek good advice on how to build a security model that is extensible and easy to read and review.

Managing the data and permission pieces separately is important from a technical perspective, but an understanding of how they all function together is even more important. Understanding the effective permissions of a user or group can reveal many data and security problems. It is very often the reflex of builders to just check boxes until something gives an expected response. If you have the team resources to specialize, separating security model builders from functional builders works well. Make your builders test the functionality of your security models as a form of quality control. Junior builders learning on the job might not understand the full breadth of implications of a security change. Your first (and most important) creations should be an effective and complete data model and security model. Next should be the processes to securely maintain and update them.

Finally, educating your in-house security team can create synergy. Show them how to probe and test security *with* you. Many organizations, even those that are making heavy use of cloud-based assets, have struggled to bring their security practices in line with modern cloud concepts. There are so many cloud providers, each with their own unique security surfaces and paradigms to understand how to secure; keeping up with even a few is challenging. Create a security review plan of items to check and investigate regularly. Schedule time for yourself to complete this process as often as you can. Invite your security peers to your review sessions. Set a separate recurring goal date to generate a summary of your findings, and another meeting to review that with technical teams and stakeholders. These meetings may be poorly attended, but you should use them as incentives to execute your plan.

Visiting your Salesforce Security Center (*https://oreil.ly/Frz8E*) can help you build and validate your plan. It assembles many pieces of information that can be used to start an investigative review process. This summary site is a great tool to share with security teams for independent inspection. If you are the person primarily responsible for the secure management of your Salesforce implementation, you'll want as many eyes on it helping you as possible.

Architects and other Salesforce adepts should bridge the gap for security stewards. Security teams that are not informed will either stifle the productivity that's possible with the platform or not protect what needs to be protected. The least transparent and open subject matter expert should shoulder the blame for breaches. It is the responsibility of the most knowledgeable to educate. Salesforce well-governed is not possible without security and compliance well-informed.

Concern: Sandbox Security

It is alarmingly easy to spin up copies of your Salesforce org. Any administrator can do it. These copies, referred to as *sandboxes*, may contain complete copies of your production data, or just a select amount of data from the parent org. Their capabilities are completely standalone, but they're still recognized as belonging to your company. Once created, the security restrictions for a sandbox can be changed, reduced, or removed altogether. Many of the largest public breaches in security have happened via non-production systems. SSO and multifactor authentication (MFA) are expensive, from a license and resource perspective, to use in every sandbox. However, if your production source code has value, then all of your sandbox orgs must be secured according to that value.

Sandboxes are valuable tools for trying new functions without impacting the production environment, especially considering the speed at which they can be created and refreshed. They're often used as playgrounds for users to learn how to use the advanced capabilities available to administrators. Care should be taken when doing this, though, as giving a user administrator rights grants them the right to create other administrator users and to expose all the data and code contained within the sandbox to anyone they like. They can bypass any and all restrictions originally put in place, like SSO and network range restrictions. Sandboxes may also not be included by default in identity management processes that deactivate former employees' accounts. These non-integrated accounts may remain active for former employees or bad actors to compromise.

Governance Strategies: Sandbox Security

Sandboxes should not be treated like playgrounds for just anyone. The free and public Salesforce training system, Trailhead, provides ample scope for those wishing to learn and experiment to do so in a safe environment. Put some educational barriers in place, and make sure users are trained on proper Salesforce usage principles before considering handing over control of a copy of your production org. Going through Trailhead training will also help introduce users to the free and safe options that are available. Because Salesforce usually includes more of the smaller developer environment creation licenses than you're ever likely to need, they can be treated as free assets to use at just about any pace.

Placing sandboxes in a secured pipeline to ensure a well-regimented development process is a very standard process. When they are respected and managed as peers to production, sandboxes are fairly easy to manage.

One of the most common patterns that is recommended but not enforced by Salesforce is to immediately clone the default System Administrator profile and remove many of the key capabilities from it. Pruning all of the dangerous permissions out of the source profile to make a safer child copy involves a decent amount of work, but as long as SSO and MFA are locked into place with other strict peripheral security components, this can be a very stable pattern for development and research.

The looser approach of letting anyone create a sandbox is doable, but it requires more oversight. Regular user rights reviews should be scheduled or scripted to ensure that no users remain in the system for much longer than necessary.

One strategy I've used in the past to secure access but keep independent processes enabled was to run a script monthly on all loose orgs that would deactivate all user accounts except for that of the person that "owned" the sandbox. The owner's password would then get reset. This meant that once a month, the owner would have to fix their password and click a few checkboxes to re-enable anyone they thought still needed access—just enough effort to get them to actually consider whether each user was worthy of being reinstated. This rather brutal approach also has the added benefit of flushing out any sandbox that has lost its owner or had its ownership unofficially transferred to someone else. Issues like these should be quickly corrected. A more likable architect might have kept a list of stakeholders and spent a considerable amount of time polling the named owners and waiting for them to reply, but shaking up access quickly brought the discussion directly to me. With appropriately justified circumstances, service could be restored in minutes.

A lot of data is automatically copied from production when a sandbox is created. You might need to tweak the migration code to filter, block, or mask sensitive data as it is brought into a sandbox with more lax controls than production. Setting up processes to custom-craft your sandboxes to be harmless environments that are unlikely to leak data can greatly decrease your high-risk attack surfaces from a security perspective. This is another really good discipline to graft into your organization as early as possible. I'm not aware of any tools that can do this automatically, by click configuration only. If someone builds something that does, buy it.

Customization

As detailed in Chapter 8, there are many options for customization within the core and extended platform components. There is also a significant amount of freedom to make a grand mess of things. Salesforce is slowly adding management features for code and automation, but there are large gaps to fill. Some of the practices you need to apply are almost a community standard at this point, but there is much that will require effective processes and determination.

In the core platform, there are two mature automation frameworks: Apex and flows. In addition, depending on how you count them, there are seven visual interface frameworks: page layouts, Lightning pages, VF pages, Aura components, LWC, screen flows, and OmniStudio. This already long list omits the mobile variants. Each of these frameworks is organized and managed in different ways. Some of them are only accessible from a code editor, and some from the web interface. Some of them are available in both. Elements of each of these frameworks can be working on the same data at the same time. Interactions and automation can include multiple instances of different components within a single page. It's fairly easy (and fun) to build these many-headed monstrosities; as usual, the hard part comes later, with maintenance and review.

Concern: Code Organization

Apex, LWC, VF, and to some extent flows have almost zero grouping controls. To use an older analogy, every file in each is in the same folder. All of them. And only sometimes are you able to sort them alphabetically. There's no way to group them, tag them, or arrange them other than by giving the files meaningful names. (Spoiler: you should give files meaningful names!) There is no requirement to how you name an Apex class or trigger file. You could create 10 different trigger code files that all run off of the action of an Account record being deleted. All your files could be named with random numbers or after your favorite Pokemon. If you have a sufficient number of developers working on your project, you *will* run into some variation of this problem. On top of that, each unit of code (component) can call other units of code in the same framework or in entirely different frameworks.

There is a primitive implementation of a "namespace" available for some types of code, but it's not always usable. It is only applicable to distributed packages. The combinatorics of all the files in each of the frameworks with varying approaches used for each adds a huge burden on newcomers trying to reverse engineer processes. Not having a clear code organization severely decreases productivity and slows time to market.

Governance Strategies: Code Organization

Start by defining a scaffolding based on capabilities. Successful enterprises manage their applications according to which of the common business capabilities they map to. I have seen several organizations utilize the map provided by LeanIX (*https://oreil.ly/Bx0yx*) (registration required) as a foundation. Once you have the major and minor functionality sketched out, you should move on to descriptive definitions. With a full set of functions and definitions, you can start to come up with naming conventions. Use your naming schema in all appropriate places, like filenames, function names, field names, and names of function-specific objects. If you are building within existing functionality that is already well defined, naming schemas are less important. Being consistent with any plan delivers most of the benefit of using one. Even a terrible naming schema, if applied consistently, is better than none at all.

Be as specific as possible when creating your functional definitions. If you start with very broad terms, getting more specific later might be a problem. It can take a lot of work to go back and correct all of the places where you've used a poorly selected name—so much work that it is seldom prioritized and done. You should do your best to get things right in the planning stage. Your choices will likely be permanent. The diagramming exercises from Figures 12-1 and 12-2 can be valuable tie-ins for your naming schema.

Avoid using branded terms or project names in naming schemas. Terms that do not directly describe the actual function of an application or set of features add an extra layer of translation. Project code names are also temporary and may be changed often. Avoid the temptation to document an acronym or abbreviation. You can abbreviate things in PowerPoint decks, emails, and other time-bound communications, but spell them out in your naming schemas and labels. Use clear, full words in code that will outlive transient messaging and work teams. If you must shorten or abbreviate words, make sure the short forms relay meaning; don't just use the catchy acronym that was used in the budget meeting. The people that will have to read your documentation and understand your application after you have been promoted will thank you for your hard work.

Another good practice can be incorporating a hierarchy into your naming schema. Try to limit the levels by using dot notation in your prefixes, with underscores (_) instead of dots. This can bring a lot of clarity. For example, HR_ONBOARD_docusign Send() and IT_ONBOARD_badgeSend() are clear method names that carry a decent amount of information. Being able to read method names and guess correctly what they do greatly shortens debugging, learning, and research times.

As a slight tangent, your functional mapping exercise is a great opportunity to find and name business stakeholder champions. Having a strong process owner and system proponent can greatly improve the perception and adoption of your platform. Building business functionality without business support is a dreary prospect. You want to build things people want to use.

Concern: Automation Orchestration

Since both Apex and flows have object triggers that can fire on record changes, it can be difficult to understand what has been triggered by what and which order they execute in. There's also a possibility that each of those flows, actions, or triggers could cause something to happen that would call another version of itself. This could lead to an infinite loop and locked records or processes. There is no automated way of tracking or dealing with these race conditions. (*Race conditions* is a name given to a problem that became common during the switch from single to multithreaded operations; code had to be refactored to handle the resource contention caused by multiple processor threads trying to lock or access the same resource at the same time.) Another analogy is order of operations in mathematics. The Apex Developer Guide (*https://oreil.ly/43rbj*) lays out the order of execution of events on the Salesforce server; this is the default path of actions that will be performed during a database transaction. But what if it doesn't work for your needs?

Governance Strategies: Automation Orchestration

You can leverage trigger-handler frameworks to organize code execution timings and helper functions. Using trigger-handler frameworks is standard practice among the Salesforce development population. The commonly accepted standard is "one trigger (file) per object." A short description of this pattern is that you designate a single file for each object to act as the controlling trigger code. Inside this single file, you designate all of the other helper functions to be called, and in what order they are called. Having just one file per object isn't mandatory, though; the important thing is to have a pattern, keep it simple, and follow it.

Many people try to apply this same pattern to flows, but because flows do have some actual restrictions on complexity, it doesn't transfer well. There are some emerging Apex trigger-handler framework patterns that attempt to incorporate flow orchestration as well; as flows gain wider adoption as a first-order tool, we should start to see more mature patterns that achieve this goal.

Concern: Nimble Versus Stable

Salesforce offers a wide variety of features and tools, and naturally many groups will want to use them—but managing different types of teams with different processes in the same organization can be a challenge. Salesforce does not have management controls that allow you to give developer-level access to only certain areas or objects. It's all or nothing. Teams or departments that want to be nimble and use simple flows, or even just add a field to a page, need full admin access. Should those simple productivity builders be forced to learn Jira and Git and staff a QA team? As that clearly wouldn't be practical, many organizations instead choose to restrict access to these features.

Governance Strategies: Time to Market Versus Stability

The best practice is to scale your change processes up according to the sensitivity of the data and the access value of the entire system. You can always make concessions for trusted partners, but those come with risks that you must accept.

Adding new developers to a shared ecosystem is great, as long as you are able to trust them to isolate risks to other processes effectively. If you have a willing and capable resource pool, turning them into citizen developers can yield significant productivity boosts. In highly technical organizations with a large pool of tech-savvy employees, a strong case can be made for a multi-org strategy for your implementation. This means that you'll be maintaining more than one independent Salesforce instance: different sets of users and potentially different components and discrete integrations. You can use one org for fast and casual goals, and another for more sensitive or critical goals. A multi-org strategy may also be appropriate if you have multiple types of highly sensitive data or processes.

Another option is allow the two different styles (fast and nimble vs. secure and stable) to work independently in different sandbox environments. Manage your nimble citizen developer org with change sets with a very limited scope in a special sandbox, and everything else via more involved change control processes. A qualified administrator will need to be in charge of merging the nimble changes into the production org. This takes additional support and buy-in from compliance teams, but it can be a good compromise to enable people. If you have team members willing to do the work to build valuable assets, find a way to say "yes." If you don't, they will likely find someone who will (or even worse, they'll stop asking). A good architect will weigh the value of the human effort required against the value of system stability and design accordingly. This is another component of the UX Architect role, which is discussed in Chapter 11.

Summary

The aim of this chapter was to outline some of the challenges you might face as a Salesforce architect as your implementation scales, and how to deal with them. Little of what we've discussed here is completely unique to Salesforce; Salesforce just has a unique assembly of quirks that require a unique application of standard management practices. There is no single recipe for how to architect the perfect system, but there are many sets of trusted heuristics and patterns that an experienced architect can apply once they can see an outline of the system. Not all of these concerns will apply to every scenario, and many are questions of scale and circumstance. It's important to be aware of the potential consequences of the changes and decisions you make as you build a system. Hopefully this chapter has provided some insight into the areas you will need to observe and some ways you can adapt as your implementation grows. An understanding of some of the governance processes that are regularly required will help you better understand the platform, as well as where and why you might need to put additional platform management practices in place. You should think of this as a starting point, however, and not an exhaustive list: you will continue to identify important architectural concerns that relate to the finer details of each system that you learn.

> Peer: Architect, what is best in life?
>
> Architect: To crush your vulnerabilities, see your outages reduced to zero, and hear the exaltation of your users.
>
> —Conan the Architect

CHAPTER 13

Roll-up and Summary

The goal of this book was to draw an outline of the shapes of the systems that are part of the Salesforce platform. We've reviewed only some of the core elements, but these are the power tools and building blocks that will comprise many of the solutions you build with Salesforce. Due to the scope and fast-changing nature of the ecosystem, I've chosen to focus on what in my experience are the most commonly used and licensed tools, and those that have the clearest analogs to existing and perhaps better-known offerings. The tools and their capabilities will change over time, as will their presentation in Salesforce's marketing materials. This book won't help you pass Salesforce exams, but it will help you understand them and start to prepare.

If you have worked with any of the major cloud providers, you understand that they have all expanded far beyond their original roles: Amazon is not just a shopping system. Microsoft doesn't just sell software. Google isn't just a search engine. Salesforce isn't just a CRM system. New capabilities continue to emerge, and the pace of evolution is staggering.

If you have a background in other technologies and systems, hopefully you are now able to see through the branding fog. There are many capabilities to harness within the Salesforce ecosystem, and equipped with an understanding of where they shine, you should do so. The architectural practices that relate to Salesforce are the same that would apply to any other system with similar characteristics. Of course, there are differences between tools and components that exist inside and outside the platform, but they are not unfathomable.

With the heavy emphasis on brand growth, you'll have to pay attention to acquisitions and evolutions—the constant naming and renaming and minor changes can make keeping track of capabilities in Salesforce a little tricky. The singular familiarity of users focused exclusively on the Salesforce platform adds to this challenge. Many practitioners have an understanding of words like "account" and "object" that is particular to the Salesforce context, and for those who aren't familiar with the platform, trying to learn new concepts or exchange ideas without an appreciation of the root definitions can slow adoption. One of the underlying goals of this book was to bridge that gap, helping users trained in Salesforce understand how its terminology and capabilities map to those of external products, while at the same time exposing those Salesforce concepts to newcomers in a relatable way. If you are specialized in Salesforce, please work to understand other systems. Better exposure and cross-platform knowledge makes for better architects.

The experienced architect will constantly strive for a better understanding of how different systems work. Every system has pros and cons, and learning about these will add to your skills. The various constraints and freedoms different product lines offer make them perfect for some jobs and ill-advised for others. Being a cross-platform architect means knowing which technology is the best choice to leverage for the problem at hand. If you don't know what else is out there, you won't deliver the optimal solution. You can do almost everything within Salesforce, but that may not always be ideal. I've seen projects fail due to architects not knowing they were doubling the cost of the solution by paying for capabilities (data storage, ETL systems, middleware, etc.) that their clients already had. Conversely, failing to understand the available ecosystem components can lead to costly missed opportunities.

Having worked with many other platforms, I can say that Salesforce is a leading solution in more than just the CRM space. It has many other capabilities that make it the right choice for many use cases. With good knowledge of what you can do with it, you can now make better decisions about when to do so.

To be fair, my love for the Salesforce ecosystem is not based only on its objective technical capabilities. Salesforce has a unique community and level of interest in its customers and experts. The company markets the successes of its big customers and of individual users, with an emphasis on sharing and encouragement. It has no equal in this regard. My career choice is heavily based on the enjoyment I get from working with the community and this spirit on a daily basis—having a career that's rewarding, not "just a job," makes it easier to tolerate long days and hard work. I am, however, still an efficient engineer, and I always aim to use the best tool for the job based on objective measures.

This book covered the Salesforce implementation of the universal concepts of functionality, data, scale, security, automation, and customization in order to share an architect's view of this platform. This perspective should help you learn and evaluate other systems, as they all share these dimensions. In my opinion the way Salesforce has combined them makes it a best-in-breed solution, but other combinations may better suit the needs of your particular project.

Thank you for taking the time to allow me to share my experiences with you. I hope this makes your journey through the Salesforce ecosystem faster and easier—and if this is your first experience with Salesforce, please let me be the first to welcome you to the Trailblazer community!

Index

About the Author

Paul McCollum is a Salesforce technical architect at Accenture. He is an original computer prodigy who started programming in the second grade, about 20 years before that became commonplace. Exposed to disruptive technology and the earliest practices of enterprise architecture, Paul has continued to work at distilling emerging technologies into their base concepts to communicate, map, and share. Over the past two decades, he has focused even more on the human side of the equation with UX and learning. Paul loves sharing technology patterns with user groups and events and has established himself as a leader, collaborator, and educator.

Colophon

The animal on the cover of *Practical Salesforce Architecture* is a thick-billed raven (*Corvus crassirostris*). These birds are some of the largest in the corvid family, and they are endemic to northeast tropical Africa.

Thick-billed ravens average between 24 and 28 inches long and can weigh between 2.5 and 3.3 pounds. They have distinctive, large, laterally compressed bills with deep curves. The bill is mostly black with a white tip. They have short feathers on their necks, throats, and heads. The feathers on their throats and upper breasts are a dark, glossy brown. The majority of a thick-billed raven's body is a glossy black with the exception of a patch of white on the back of the neck. This species has strong legs and feet that are also black.

Thick-billed ravens are omnivores and scavengers at heart, eating grubs, beetle larvae, carrion, bird eggs, rodents, lizards, plant matter, and human food. Vultures, impressed by this raven's big bills, will make space for thick-billed ravens when scavenging a carcass. The ravens use a scything method with their beaks to break apart dung so they can eat the grubs.

The preferred habitat of thick-billed ravens is mountains and high plateaus at elevations of 1,500 to 3,400 meters in Eritrea, Ethiopia, Somalia, and Sudan. They can be found in a range of biomes, such as forests, grasslands, rocky areas, and even cities and towns with large trees.

Thick-billed ravens have a stable population and are categorized as a species of Least Concern on endangered species lists. However, many of the animals on O'Reilly covers are endangered; all of them are important to the world.

The cover is a color illustration by Karen Montgomery, based on a black and white engraving from Lydekker's *Royal Natural History*. The cover fonts are Gilroy Semibold and Guardian Sans. The text font is Adobe Minion Pro; the heading font is Adobe Myriad Condensed; and the code font is Dalton Maag's Ubuntu Mono.

O'REILLY®

Learn from experts.
Become one yourself.

Books | Live online courses
Instant answers | Virtual events
Videos | Interactive learning

Get started at oreilly.com.

Printed in the USA
CPSIA information can be obtained
at www.ICGtesting.com
JSHW052019130524
63048JS00008B/392

9 781098 138288